A Doctor in the House

A Doctor in the House

MY LIFE WITH
BEN CARSON

CANDY CARSON

Sentinel

SENTINEL

An imprint of Penguin Random House LLC
375 Hudson Street
New York, New York 10014
penguin.com

Photographs courtesy of the author unless otherwise indicated.

ISBN 978-1-59523-124-6

Printed in the United States of America
1   3   5   7   9   10   8   6   4   2

Set in Ehrhardt MT Std
Designed by Leonard Telesca

This book is gratefully dedicated to Sonya Carson, Ben's mother, and to my parents, Samuel and Cerise Rustin, who through their sacrificial and loving guidance used their knowledge, wisdom, and experience to shape Ben and me into who we are.

Contents

A Doctor in the House

Introduction

"Wake up! Ben! *Ben! Wake uhhh . . .*"

Horrific pain shot through my midsection, abruptly silencing my frantic cries. It radiated to the extremities of my thirty-nine-week-pregnant body as I tried to breathe. It was two a.m., and Ben, coming off another rough week, was sleeping deeply and not responding to my desperate pleas. Prior to this particular night, I had found it amusing that he could wake from a sound sleep at a single ring of the telephone or beep of a beeper, but with any other sound, even when our first baby son would cry, Ben would be the one sleeping like a baby! He called it "selective hearing for medical survival." I'm not sure I believed him, but it sounded good.

Only it didn't sound so good as the pain started up again. The contractions were unexpected because I still had one more week to go and the first baby had taken a full forty weeks. Yet here I was in the midst of what I knew had to be labor, and because the contractions were just under two minutes apart, I was thinking this was, to put it mildly, *not good*!

On the next break from the pain, I managed to make my way to the bathroom, getting there just before another contraction hit. Calling out from the well-lit bathroom to the still-darkened bedroom, the message finally reached Ben's subconscious.

Once awake, Ben went into doctor mode, though he didn't yet realize how advanced my labor was. "Are you sure the baby's coming? How close are the contractions? When did they start?" he called from the bedroom. Still trying to catch my breath, I couldn't answer right away, but thank God for Lamaze! The breathing rehearsals from those classes kicked in and did their job! When I had breath enough to answer, I realized that not only was the baby coming, he was actually here!

"Honey, I think you better check," I replied. And sure enough, little BJ was there. Ben dashed into the bathroom just in time to catch BJ before he fully emerged, holding the baby in one hand while he caught the afterbirth in the other. The emergency was not over yet, though, because the umbilical cord needed to be clamped. Ben literally had his hands full, so he told me to find something to clip off the placenta.

Considering I had just given birth, this might be considered a bit much to ask, but it had to be done, because the placenta contained the baby's wastes, and it would be unhealthy for that to flow back to the baby. Fortunately, since the labor had taken less than an hour I was able to move around without too much difficulty. I ran up and down stairs looking for anything that might work, peering into drawers, checking on shelves, using my imagination to conjure up an answer to the problem as I searched the entire house, along with Ben's mother, who was staying with us to help. Ben was calling out potential solutions, suggesting clothespins and other items—but I knew there weren't any clothespins in the house, because we had a clothes dryer even back then.

Suddenly, rummaging through a drawer, I found a roller clip, the kind that is shaped like a bobby pin, only with straight shafts. I ran back up the stairs to where Ben had the baby, and he clipped off the umbilical, gave a sigh of relief, and must have cleaned the baby up. I don't know exactly what happened next, because by that time the fire department had come and I had to answer the door. The startled firemen instructed me to take my place on the stretcher. I politely told them I'd been up and down the stairs several times and really didn't need one. "I can walk just fine," I said. They countered with "This is 'procedure,' ma'am," but they finally offered an alternative: a seated stretcher, much like a sedan chair that carries royalty in the old films. It was great fun being carried around like a movie star!

In one sense, BJ's birth is the story of our life in a nutshell. From the day I met Ben, he has come through for me in difficult situations. The life of a neurosurgeon isn't an easy one, and like others he has been called to go above and beyond the call of duty almost constantly. The life of a neurosurgeon's wife isn't much easier, and I've had to put up with challenges that most wives don't face. But it's all been worth it. Together, we've been through poverty, tragedy, disappointments, joy, successes, and wealth. Even when things have been hard, we've had each other's backs. I can't help but admire and cherish a man who always puts others first. I love this guy.

Chapter 1

College and Meeting Ben

When I left home after high school graduation, the anticipation of new learning experiences thrummed through my veins. The excitement of going off to college, of being on my own, thrilled me. What freedom to make decisions all on my own, what power, answering only to myself! But it was a bit scary, too, no longer having the immediate gentle counsel of my parents! What if I made a mistake?

I had no plans to marry a doctor when I headed off to college. As a kid from inner-city Detroit, I had stayed pretty close to the neighborhood I'd grown up in before going to New Haven. When I first arrived on Yale's campus in the fall of 1971, I was amazed, astonished, filled with wide-eyed wonder. I dutifully read all the handouts for new students to make sure I was up on things and had an understanding of what was required, but the sheer magnitude of this adventure was somewhat mind-boggling! But I kept my astonishment to myself. As a freshman, I wanted to act cool, like this was everyday stuff.

It wasn't that my parents hadn't tried to give me a breadth of experience, but we were from a pretty humble background. The daughter of a Floridian physician and nurse, my mother was orphaned at age twelve and was raised by her great-uncle and -aunt in Detroit. She had finished high school at fifteen and started college right away, becoming a teacher and later marrying my father, who worked in an automobile factory in Detroit.

Born Lacena Rustin, I was the third of my parents' five children. Linzy was the oldest, followed by Cerise, then came me, and Del was the youngest. I arrived at a time when my mother was working to provide a stable home life for her family. My father was an alcoholic, something Mom wasn't aware of when they married, because during their dating period she saw him only when he was on leave from the army and he was on his best behavior. Dad's addiction forced him to drop out of pharmacy school, but by the time I was two years old, he had realized how destructive alcohol was and joined Alcoholics Anonymous. We hosted AA meetings at our home regularly and Dad never took another drink.

When I was three, my baby sister, Sinena, a year younger than Del, died in a fire, a tragedy that must have really shaken my parents, but my childhood was pleasant despite the tragedy, and the addiction issue had been resolved by the time I might have noticed. Dad was a family man who didn't mind playing with us and made us kids all feel special. He would hold our hands as we attended parent/teacher conferences while Mom was involved in her own at her school. And Dad was a great cook. He could take chicken and make it so tender and flavorful it would make you cry for mercy. Best of all, Dad was my hero for sneaking me candy. Mom didn't like us having too much, but Dad would provide me with treats from time to time because he knew how much I liked them. He started calling me his "candy," and the name stuck.

The sweet tooth that earned me my nickname didn't change. From the time I was about eleven on, as one of our chores, my sister Cerise and I would take turns baking cakes for the AA meetings. I liked baking but didn't appreciate my mother's rule that we couldn't eat the fruits of our labors. I realize now, and probably knew subconsciously back then, that she only had my best interests at heart as I was a chubby kid. But it just didn't seem fair that we had to go through all that work baking from scratch and mixing the icing from powdered sugar and butter and not even getting a little taste. We were obedient kids, though, and the rules ruled.

In fact, Cerise was always willing to do whatever helped to keep the peace. I recall one time when we were being babysat at the home of some of our parents' friends, and the lady of the house required that we go to bed by seven p.m. Cerise wasn't my senior by much, but she was allowed to stay up a whole extra hour later than our little brother, Del, and me. The injustice of having to go to bed an hour earlier than our sister (when we usually all went to bed at the same time) seemed so unfair. And because we were allowed to watch television, something that was a very limited treat at home, it simply didn't seem right that Cerise should have an extra hour to watch while we didn't. Del and I of course protested our bedtime quite vigorously, but our hostess was firm in her decision. So Cerise, with her giving, sacrificial spirit, said she would go to bed at the same time as we did even though she could have watched TV an hour longer. That attitude was typical of her and she has been a terrific role model for me as well as a great best friend.

Mom was very practical and organized things so that no one person in the family had too much to do. We divided up chores, taking turns preparing Dad's morning coffee the night before by filling the water reservoir and inserting the filter with the required amount of coffee grounds, so that all he had to do was plug it in once he came into the kitchen. We helped Mom with her classroom bulletin boards, setting up her classroom at the beginning of the year and moving out at the end of the year. We even helped her with grading math and science papers from the time we were in upper elementary school.

As a result of her efforts, my first paycheck came from the Detroit Board of Education. Mom had needed someone to sketch historical figures on mimeograph sheets so that she could reproduce them for her class—photocopiers weren't yet widely used. Because I had taken art classes, Mom got me hired. It was cool to be paid for something I enjoyed doing, and really exciting to know I had earned my own money. I quickly envisioned spending sprees. But my mother gave me another vision—a reality check—and informed me that the money would go toward college.

Chores were shared, and once they were done we could take advantage of the many freebies available in the city. Mom felt she had missed out as a child and was committed to introducing us to as many experiences to broaden our horizons as possible, as long as they were free or close to it. The neighborhood recreation center was one of our "hot spots," and it was there that my sister and I took ballet and tap dancing, and I learned leather craft.

Football games were free because we lived behind the high school. Dad would park Betsy the car—a big black Buick hardtop—under the cherry tree in our backyard, and we kids would sit on top and watch the end of the field that we could see. The rest of the field was hidden behind the bleachers, but we didn't care. Sometimes we'd even have popcorn. And Dad always let us name our cars. The last one was a Mercury we bought in 1965 which was so sleek, we called it "Hot 25."

Although Mom's primary source of income was from teaching,

she also was our church organist, and as such required that each of us learn piano and at least one other instrument. Dad even played piano some too. And she made sure we were kept busy with orchestras. At one point in high school she was driving me to rehearsals for three different orchestras besides the two that I played in at my school.

With my mother being a teacher, of course bad grades just were not acceptable. Our parents set the bar high and we had to get the best grades. We practically lived at the library, we visited there so often. And as a teacher, she also helped us to understand that "teachers are people too." On Valentine's Day, Christmas, and other holidays, while most kids would make cards for their friends, we made cards for the teachers and administrators because they might be left out.

Mom and Dad believed in service as well. Every Sunday, when Dad would make coffee for early service at church, he had us take turns measuring the coffee grounds, because he wanted us to learn to help out in the church. We also helped with other church functions like pancake suppers and Vacation Bible School. From the time we were young, Mom would volunteer herself and us for programs around the city and get us in free, and sometimes we could take home extras of the treats that had been distributed to guests at special programs. Because we all played instruments, she would take us to nursing homes and play for the residents there. Later on after Dad succumbed to cancer, Mom even became the chaplain at several nursing homes.

Because Mom taught science and math, we all had some interest in those subjects and some experience with grading papers in them. As a result, it was sort of natural for me to choose premed as a focus for my college studies, though I wasn't committed to a medical career. By the time I got accepted to Yale, I was simply tired of people asking me what I was going to do. In high school everyone takes the basics, but there's not much opportunity to try a lot of different things. That's what college is for; with so many classes in so many disciplines, students can explore various subjects to determine where their talents really lie. So I figured if people asked about my major, I'd just respond "premed," and go on about my business. I wouldn't be stuck trying to explain, "Well, I haven't quite decided yet," or "I haven't found my niche yet," or "I can't make up my mind." And I liked science anyway, so I started out with science courses, which turned out to be quite a bit of fun, by the way.

The Wonders of New Haven

Yale itself was a huge adjustment. On the college campus were gorgeous architectural styles of periods I had only seen in books. Exotic foods were the norm. Or perhaps I should say, expensive foods that we had never even read about, like London broil and Cornish hens. This was a stark contrast to the frozen bags of mixed vegetables that were a staple in our household. Because both my parents worked, they were usually exhausted when they got home and the meals were quick, easy fixes, for time at home was limited, but on weekends Dad treated us with his specialties.

College was a "land of wonder" I had to take in, and I tried to get over the amazement of it quickly so I could apply myself to the job at hand: studying. Sterling Library was another architectural wonder, packed with books of all shapes, sizes, subjects, and interesting covers and bindings. Some were done in leather with brass clasps, others had metal corners on tooled, embossed leather covers. I recall having difficulty concentrating while attempting to study in the stacks, as I would discover even more of these uniquely designed book covers.

In the dining halls, we folks from the ghettos of America found it was wise to listen first to the conversations around the table before saying anything. We wanted to find out what was the prevailing attitude of those who had been more privileged growing up, so we could fit in. But it wasn't long before we discovered that virtually everyone was searching for purpose and meaning in life. The questions "Who am I, really?," "Why am I here on this earth?," and "What is my real purpose in life?" came up time and again as students finally had enough free time on their hands to relax from school duties, household chores, jobs, et cetera, to consider the seemingly elusive "ultimate reality." All of us were seeking answers.

Sometimes the people we asked for those answers didn't always guide us correctly. A word of caution to those who go to institutions of higher learning. I had a few questions with respect to credits and requirements for students with more than one major, so I made an appointment to see my counselor. His office was what you'd expect with a desk loaded with piles of papers, bookcases filled with references, et cetera. He was cordial and seemed genuinely interested in my goals and aspirations. At the end of the meeting I felt well armed with his advice to tackle the challenges ahead. But a little voice in the back of my mind told me to check a few other sources to make sure that I was headed in the right direction. I didn't want to make any big mistakes when it came to preparing for my eventual graduation. I really was quite shocked when I discovered that he not only didn't answer my questions appropriately, but that the information he gave me was exactly the opposite of what was required. So when you ask advice, please double-check either with others from that department or other departments that interface with that one. Your time is limited (and costs money!) and you don't want to waste it by doing the wrong thing to accomplish your goals!

I was happy to make it through my first year, and then, in the midst of all the continued unsettled questioning during my sophomore year, I noticed that there were two students who always appeared to have their act together and to have already found their purpose. They were confident, self-assured, and comfortable in their own skins, which drew me like a moth to a flame. These students were Ben Carson and his roommate Larry Harris. They were both premed seniors and were truly "easy on the eyes" handsome. And they didn't mind talking to me, a mere sophomore! Many upperclassmen would just brush by those of us with less college experience, but these two always said hello when they saw me. I was flattered and intrigued and decided I wanted to learn what made these two men different.

Extracurricular Activities with Ben

One time as I was walking back to the residence hall from class, I ran into Ben and his roommate going in the same direction. After general greetings and questions about classes, the conversation turned to music. When they asked me if I knew anyone who played the organ, I admitted I had filled in for my mom at church back home from time to time and had played at my high school baccalaureate. They then explained the reason for the question. The church they attended needed an alternate choir organist, and as representatives of the choir (Ben sang bass and Larry sang tenor) they asked if I would like to try out. After a short pause, I replied that I would try, but that I hadn't played in a while.

The audition did not go well. I had no organ to practice on and hadn't played in more than a year, so it showed. I was embarrassed,

but both Ben and Larry were perfect gentlemen. Neither laughed—
at least not out loud. And the organist who was in charge of the
audition was very tactful, recalling that I hadn't had a chance to
practice much and suggesting that perhaps I might enjoy singing
with the choir. I eagerly accepted, and, well, what a treat that was.
You always hear of how "the whole is more than the sum of the
parts," but to actually see (or hear) it in action is quite a marvelous
revelation. So I continued going to choir rehearsals on Friday nights
with the guys, as well as Bible study (Sabbath school) and church
on Saturday.

The Bible study was completely refreshing. Learning directly
from the Holy Book was not only enlightening but fulfilling. Most
times in our church back home, biblical principles and precepts
were interpreted and disseminated by the minister. But the regular
practice of studying the Bible, discovering the truths more experi-
entially with a subject guide, was new to me. The Seventh-day Adventist Church publishes daily Bible study guides for each quarter
of the year, commonly called "quarterlies." These are distributed a
week or so before they are current to give everyone a chance to
prepare for the week's lesson. I thoroughly appreciated the focused commentary of the booklets and was also impressed with the
seriousness and dedication with which the parishioners attempted
to follow what was learned. Worship service was somewhat different from what I had grown up with as well. The liturgy was not the
same weekly verbiage interspersed with intoned chants that I was
used to. The service progressed with more congregational involvement in a less formal format.

When I asked what makes the Seventh-day Adventist Church
different from others, the answer was always the same: "Seventh-
day Adventists take into consideration the whole Bible and don't

leave out any parts, or try to change any." And the church is called Seventh-day Adventist in keeping with the sabbath that God observed in Genesis 2, which was confirmed as a sign between God and His people in Exodus 20. It all made sense to me, so I decided to join the church.

Typically on a Saturday morning, Ben, Larry, and I would ride to church on the bus, or sometimes one of the members would pick us up from campus. It was a wonderful break from the rigors of academia. Lifting our voices together in praise by singing hymns, having lively Bible discussions, and in general, worshipping and fellowshipping with like-minded believers was a greatly relaxing and enjoyable way to recharge for the next week.

The first time I recall witnessing Ben saving a life was one such Sabbath at the church we attended in Hamden, Connecticut, about twenty minutes' drive from the college campus. The service had started and all the preliminaries had been completed. Announcements, the first hymn, prayer and scripture readings had all been done and we had settled back for the wise words of the week. Gazing forward and taking in the homily, Ben and I figured that poor Larry must have had a hard week, for he had fallen asleep. The little snores he emitted were what tipped us off. At first we were the only ones who noticed, but as his snoring increased in volume, he drew the attention of a no-nonsense church lady seated next to us. Her wide-brimmed, floral-trimmed hat bobbed indignantly as she prepared to give him what looked like it would be a sizable wallop. Before she could connect her ample arms with Larry's person, Ben quickly but gently shook Larry's shoulder, whispering urgently, "Larry, if you value your life, you'd better wake up." Larry kept his eyes open for the rest of church that day.

As most young ladies do when they begin to notice a guy with "potential," I thought there might be possibilities. His confidence, leadership qualities, and calm demeanor were attractive, and the fact that he was a handsome dude wasn't lost on me either. However, it wasn't long before my hopes for the "potential" I had seen were dashed and I was disabused of the idea that we could be more than casual friends. He and his best buddy, Larry, were generally kind, considerate, and respectful and treated me as an intellectual equal, but there was one serious drawback. They enjoyed teasing me by calling me names, often in other languages. Perhaps they thought it was all in fun, but it certainly was not amusing, fun, or anything like that for me! It never occurred to me that the gibes that so bothered me might be signs of affection. Fortunately, the benefits I got from going to their church were so important to me that I just decided I'd turn a deaf ear to their taunts and enjoy the new approach to spiritual education that was now available.

Ben's Background

I wasn't the only person who was impressed by Ben Carson. It was pretty clear to anyone who knew Ben in college that he was special. Even as a child, Ben had the desire to be the best he could be, and his dedication to excellence had carried him far. Though I knew little about his childhood when I first met him, I could see the fruits of his mother's discipline in the way he carried himself and as they were revealed in his own high standards even before I knew the stories of events that had shaped him.

One story I would later learn from Ben's older brother, Curtis, perfectly encapsulated Ben's competitive nature. Concerned for her sons' education, Ben's devoted mother, Sonya Carson, had required that the boys read and report on two books each week.

Once she had laid the law down about going to the library, the boys would make that trip virtually every day, and it was a "good little hike," Curtis remarked. "Ben had somewhat of a competitive nature and could make a game out of almost anything." As the two of them would cross the streets on the way to school or anywhere else, Curtis noticed (but Ben wasn't aware he had noticed) the way Ben would time his steps so that his foot would touch the opposite curb as they crossed before Curtis's foot would. Ben never mentioned it nor was he overt in the manner in which he performed this challenge, but every single time they would cross a street Ben had to get there first. And in general, Curtis said, he always seemed to manage things so they would come out the way he wanted them to. That desire to be the best still resides within his chest.

Ben was a stickler for being on time as well. Curtis remembers that when their mother required them to be back home by a certain hour, Ben would calculate the time it took to get from there to their destination to make sure he knew exactly when to leave to keep their promise. So when they were allowed to go play baseball, Ben kept a close eye on his watch as they made their way over, to determine exactly how long it took to walk from home to the ball field. All the kids would be seriously playing, making their long-reach catches, getting as many hits as possible, and running bases like their lives depended on it. But when the calculated time came to leave, Ben would stop whatever he was in the middle of and start walking home. It didn't matter if it was in the middle of an inning or if he was at bat, he was not going to disappoint his mother. Poor Curtis would try to at least finish out the inning to be fair to his team, and then would run to catch up to Ben. His worst fear was that Ben might see a big dog, run out into the street to get away from it, and get hit by a car. And Curtis knew he needed to be home at the same time or at least close to the time Ben arrived so he wouldn't be considered guilty of not keeping an eye on his younger brother.

In New Haven it was the same. Ben always arrived five to ten minutes ahead of time for everything, including class, his job, church, and social meetings. He would rather be early than late. In the movie *Gifted Hands*, which chronicles his life, he is shown being almost late for class, but that didn't happen in real life. Even when someone ran a red light, crashing into and totaling his car near the hospital on his way to work in March 2012, he still got to the OR in time to do his surgery.

Perfection?

Some might wish I could point out Ben's flaws from those early years to balance out his virtues, but the truth is that I can't think of anything. Other than the incessant teasing, which did drive me up the wall, Ben is the closest to perfection that I can imagine. He was and is a very devout believer in Christ and maintains and protects that relationship with God diligently. One "fault" one might say he has is that sometimes he's so focused on what he's doing that he doesn't see what might be right in front of him. For example, if I'm looking for a missing item, like my glasses or a file of papers, sometimes it's right before his eyes. He was just too focused on what he was doing to notice it right away. So there are two rules in our house. Rule number 1: If you really want a message to get through, say it three times. Rule number 2: If you hear something three times don't get upset—it's the rule.

Curtis also recalls that he had no memory of Ben ever being seriously punished. He seemed to learn from his big brother's mistakes. But one time when Ben was in the third grade and felt he had really gotten into big trouble at school, he came home at lunchtime because school was so close, and started rummaging through the garage. "Curtis, have you seen the rat poison?" Ben's query brought the response "No. But why would you want rat poison?" Ben said, "I'm looking for the best way to kill myself. Something bad happened at school, and there's no other way out of this." Curtis made an effort to look thoughtful for a few seconds while his mind reeled with horror at what Ben was trying to do, and said as nonchalantly as possible, "Well, there's a much better way to do it, if you really want it done right." "And what's that?" Ben eagerly asked. As solemnly as he could muster, Curtis counseled, "You have to drink a lot of water . . . a LOT OF WATER. You keep drinking and drinking until you finally burst."

Ben couldn't help but question him again: "Are you sure this will work? Is this really the best way?" and Curt reassured Ben in typical big brother fashion, "Oh yeah! I know for a fact that this is absolutely the best way to do it!" So obedient little Ben drank . . . and drank . . . and drank . . . and continued to faithfully drink (as well as go to the bathroom—he said the liquid was coming out almost as quickly as it was going in). He continued until late in the afternoon, when he realized it wasn't worth the effort. Fortunately, by the time I met Ben ten years later, he had been eager to live again for quite a while.

When Curtis joined the ROTC in high school, he didn't think Ben had even noticed. Curt first saw it as a nice alternative to gym class, and after reading about West Point in the books his mom had required them to go through from the library, a career in the military had become his goal. The uniforms, parades, and medals drew him in. He had set another strong example for his brother, and Ben decided to join the ROTC after his first semester in high school.

Well, once again, when Ben joined, he wanted to be the best. The highest rank a student could earn was colonel, and the highest ROTC rank for a student in the city of Detroit would be the city executive officer. Ben was thinking, "Wow! What if I could make it all the way to the top!" This was a feat that typically required six full semesters, the last three years of high school. So it didn't seem possible because he had started a whole semester late (in the second half of his sophomore year instead of at the beginning). But you should never say "never."

Shortly after he joined, a unique opportunity was posed to Ben by one of the advisers, who recognized Ben's ambition. There was a second-period ROTC class that was, to put it mildly, quite unruly. It seemed no one could manage to keep them in line or get them to cooperate in any way. The ROTC adviser said, "Carson, if you can do something with this class, I'll promote you all the way to second lieutenant." The gauntlet was down now. Starting like all new recruits as a buck private, by his second semester Ben had already progressed quickly through several ranks and was a sergeant first class. He would be able to reach in two semesters what usually takes three to four and all he had to do was work with one class. Based on this success, he was thinking, "Piece of cake." But he hadn't seen this class, and when he did, he realized precisely why the adviser was so generous with his offer. The class was completely out of control. And every other phrase out of the students' mouths was "I'm gonna kick your . . . !"

In talking with the students in that class, Ben discovered the students' affinity for guns and knives, and decided to take advantage of that interest. He began to practice rifle drills with them, teaching them how to assemble and disassemble the weapons, the proper ways to hold and position the weapons, et cetera. It wasn't long before they were the top drill team in the entire school. Ben had met the challenge and attained the rank that was high enough for him to qualify to take the field grade exam and possibly earn an even higher rank. Each time the opportunity came to take the field grade exam, he studied hard and achieved the highest score. By the time he was in the middle of his senior year, he had already reached his goal of becoming the highest-ranking ROTC officer in the school, a full colonel. And he still had a semester left.

By scoring the highest mark in the city on the last field grade exam, he then became the highest-ranking student ROTC officer in the entire city of Detroit, more than twenty-two high school ROTC units. And as such he had wonderful opportunities to meet people like General William Westmoreland, attend a Congressional Medal of Honor dinner, march in the front of parades, et cetera.

Considering his meager beginnings, who couldn't help but admire such a paragon of virtue?

Up for a Challenge

After meeting Ben, I discovered he was always up for a challenge—it almost didn't matter what the task was. While we were in college, he discovered foosball and became obsessed. At Yale there were twelve residential colleges, each of which had lodging for students with a central courtyard, dining hall, and some sort of amusement for the students, such as ping-pong, billiards, et cetera. Ben's residential college was Davenport, which happened to have a foosball table. With foosball, as with just about any other activity Ben got involved in, he wanted to be the best, practicing during his free time in between study periods and classes. It wasn't long before not only was he the champion, but the regulars actually named a unique maneuver after him. It was a lightning-fast shot Ben had developed that left most people wondering what had happened.

Ben's confidence in another "sport" really amazed me and some of his peers as well. The first American-born world chess champion, Bobby Fischer, attained that title in 1972 when he was twenty-nine. As a senior, Ben was only twenty-one, but he planned on challenging Fischer. Wow! Was I impressed! Much later I discovered Ben's kidding sense of humor with respect to Fischer. He could say the most outrageous things with a straight face, and some of us would believe him.

Ben the Cop

Neither Ben nor I had much extra money in college. I sometimes played gigs with my violin to earn some cash. To supplement his income, Ben had a part-time job on campus. He was a student police aide. The trustworthiness of candidates for this position was a principal requirement. The job didn't involve patrolling the campus as much as it did ensuring that buildings were secure. So he was entrusted with a set of keys for opening the required buildings for events or student meetings, and locking up afterward. The walkie-talkie he carried kept him informed of the times to carry out his duties. Once when he was attending a Black Students at Yale (BSAY) meeting, he was on duty and his walkie-talkie crackled to life. He quickly turned it down as just about all the students looked around to see who the campus-cop-spy was. There was no police uniform in sight, so no one figured it out.

The thought that he could get into any concert he wanted to free of charge, or utilize any of the rooms on campus for personal gain, never even tempted him. He did his job, did not abuse his authority, and after handing in the keys from his shift, went straight back to his residential hall to study. Overall, he was a responsible, trustworthy young man, the kind of person you don't mind including in your circle of friends.

Despite his teasing, we continued to grow in friendship. I had never really had any close friends who were boys, so this was a unique experience, one that was not unpleasant. Little did I know that our friendship would soon go further.

Chapter 2

Falling in Love?

Several months into my sophomore year and Ben's senior year, the teasing from him and Larry was just a fact of life, and school had become a routine: go to classes, do your homework, do your laundry, repeat ad infinitum.

From our point of view, life had become just a tad—not a lot, mind you, but just a tad—boring. We didn't know any better, so we complained that things were not as exciting as they could have been, thinking a little adventure might be nice. Be careful what you wish for! Sometimes you get what you ask for, and it's not what you expected.

In November, with Thanksgiving just around the corner, the Yale campus was abuzz with students looking forward to getting away from the stress of studying to enjoy the holiday. But Ben and I, along with a few other students in similar financial situations, expected to be left behind on the deserted campus. We simply could not afford to spend precious dollars on airfare to go home for only a few days. Christmas break was coming up next month, and each of our budgets could handle only one round trip home during the school year. Even flying standby was not enough of a discount to make a second trip affordable.

But this year we were in luck. Yale offered to cover travel expenses for minority students who would recruit for them in their home states over Thanksgiving break. The plan was to send a guy and a girl to each area, and I was thrilled when I was chosen to be the female representative to Detroit. The only problem was, I was going to be stuck with Ben, who still teased me mercilessly to the point where I pretty much went to church regardless of him and his taunts. I didn't mind being friends with him, but he was just too silly for me to have serious thoughts about. Fortunately, my appreciation for the opportunity to go home and visit family overrode my trepidation at having to spend almost an entire week with this dude. How he felt about spending time with me, I didn't know.

We could have flown back to Detroit for the holiday, but Ben loved driving—he grew up in the Motor City, after all. He figured he'd save the school some expenses by renting a car and driving the entire distance. I didn't particularly like the idea of spending that many hours with Ben—remember, this guy teased me ALL the time—so I was relieved when circumstances forced me to fly. It turned out that I had to perform with the Yale Symphony the weekend he was driving out, so I ended up taking a plane on the Monday of Thanksgiving week and meeting Ben at the first target school, Southwestern High.

Southwestern High was Ben's former high school, and my sister was actually doing an internship there on her way to becoming a counselor. Ben and I agreed to keep our trip quiet, so it could be a surprise when we arrived, but you know what they say about the best-laid plans. Gosh darn it, if she didn't check the guest roster for the day and spot our names before we even walked in the door. We were busted. But we enjoyed our time together there.

That week, Ben and I visited three schools each day, acquainting high school students with our perspectives on the great institution of learning that Yale is. In between high schools we would go to lunch and chat about the schools and potential candidates, comparing notes and preparing a report for Yale with recommendations for applicants.

Because Ben was the upperclassman, he was in control of the travel funds. Some evenings, we would go to a movie or other amusement, and my thought was "He's being a little loose with the school's money," not realizing he had asked me out on dates and was paying for the evening outings out of his own pocket. I didn't call him on the spending (until much later), because the outings were something fun to do, and it was a nice change to be with him without being teased. He was actually likable. What a novel thought!

Not realizing Ben was interested in me, I was impressed at how much interest he took in my relatives. Ben was friendly to my family, especially to my mom's guardian, Uncle Moses, who lived in Detroit. When Ben picked me up from my granduncle's house on the weekend, after I'd visited there during the day, they started a conversation that led to their speaking in French. After serving in World War I, Uncle Moses had stayed in Europe and studied at the University of Toulouse in France, obtaining a teaching certificate, so he spoke French fluently. When he returned to America, he would have taught, but a black teacher's salary was much less than that of a factory job, so he worked in the factory to support his family, including my mom and her brother, whom he raised. He never lost his love of French or teaching, however, and taught us grandnieces and -nephews and the neighborhood kids as much as he could. He was absolutely delighted to speak with Ben in his other language while I finished getting ready to go.

Later that weekend, after some discussion, Ben and I decided that we wanted to spend the last night in our home state at the University of Michigan, even though traveling to Ann Arbor would add an extra hour of travel time to the journey back to Yale. The travel time didn't faze us, because we were each excited to spend an evening at the place where Ben planned on going to medical school. I was eager to spend the night with my sister, who was studying there, and Ben had a close friend that he stayed with. We were so excited, in fact, that like most young people, we thought we were invincible, and we stayed up all night long, talking with our family and friends. This did not bode well for the trip home.

The next day, we started our drive back. Our energy was not at 100 percent, but we felt like we could make it. Driving during the day wasn't so bad, but we were in trouble as it got dark. Most young parents notice early on that the motion of the car is an excellent way to put babies and children to sleep, especially when nothing else works, and Ben and I weren't exactly unwilling to sleep. Ben and I intended to get that car back to New Haven before the school would be charged for another day's rental, but "the spirit was willing, but the flesh was weak," as the church folks say. We had the radio turned up high, we had the windows opened enough for a refreshing breeze, and we tried everything we knew to stay awake. But our tired, sleep-deprived bodies just would not cooperate, especially with that gentle motion of the car. Near Youngstown, Ohio, on November 28, on Interstate 80,

we both fell asleep . . . at ninety miles per hour . . .
on the highway . . . in the dead of night. THE END

Or it should have been the end for us!

The car started to vibrate as the wheels crunched the gravel on the shoulder next to the road. As we both were so rudely awakened from our naps, Ben with his quick reflexes whipped the steering wheel to the left to keep from going into the drainage ditch. By all laws of physics, that car should have gone end over end at that speed. Instead, it went around in a circle several times, as if it were on a compact Indy 500 track. And then it stopped, facing in the right direction and in the right lane. Ben said he had *not* touched the brakes.

As we caught our breath, we noticed an eighteen-wheeler barreling up behind us and Ben pulled over onto the shoulder and parked. I think God's ears were burning, we were sending up so many thank-yous! When we settled down enough to pray more calmly, we thanked God again for sparing our lives, especially when it was our negligence over sleep that caused the problem. And we knew then that God had something special in store for us. We had no clue what it was, but we decided then and there to celebrate every month on the 28th the amazing fact that He had spared our lives. We celebrated our 510th month-e-versary on May 28, 2015. To this day we never complain about being bored or lacking adventure.

Growing in Faith

When we returned to the university, we also returned to our routines: go to class, study and do homework, do laundry and repeat. One thing was different this time, though, as I began to seriously consider the lessons of all the Bible study classes I had attended at the church in Connecticut. The people there really made me feel welcome. I really never felt like an outsider, but it seemed something was still missing. And then one day it hit me: I had not taken that final step, the one where you finally realize Who the Source of all life and love and everything good in life really is. That step where you decide that you would rather have freedom of choice in Jesus than be bound by human vices and tendencies. All those things you seem to have control over and then lose control of can be overcome with His help. So I decided to get baptized, and as a result of that decision began special studies, meeting with a Bible teacher from church at the site every Wednesday evening.

The amazing thing to me was that Ben would accompany me to these classes. He already knew this stuff! But he would ride the bus with me, and we'd wait outside the church until the teacher came. He'd even stay through the entire lesson! He was a senior, and it was January of his last term, so his load was somewhat lighter than in the past, but I knew he still had plenty of work to finish. I started to wonder again what his motives were because I had never had that kind of sacrificial support from any friends in my life before this. Family sacrifices for you, as my sweet sister demonstrated quite often as we grew up. But such dedication from a friend? I had been a loner most of my life because I was one of the smart kids whom others made fun of. The one close girlfriend in high school who was also a high academic achiever was as supportive of me as I was of her, but she wouldn't have been supportive to that degree. Ben's sacrifice of his time and energies was not one that was easy for me to understand, given my background.

When I finally confronted him—"Why are you being so nice to me?"—I imagined he was going to come back in a deep voice with something like, "You know, baby, I love you." Remember, this guy is from "the Hood" in Detroit. But instead he shyly said, in a soft and sincere voice, "Because I like you." His sweet little heart was on his sleeve, and my heart melted.

Once we were "going together," we were pretty much inseparable. We'd meet for breakfast at our dining hall, treasuring the times we got to eat by ourselves, but sometimes eating with other friends. Then we'd walk together toward our first class of the day, separating only when the pathway to our classes required it. Most times we would meet for lunch at a dining hall near the next class or midway between our classes if they were a distance apart. We enjoyed studying together, particularly at Cross Campus, the underground library centrally located at the school. There were modular overstuffed cubic seats that were too comfortable for me—too easy to fall asleep in—but the desks along the walls were perfect. We'd sit at adjacent desks, time our study periods, try to focus on the project at hand without watching the clock, and take our scheduled breaks together with a trip to the water fountain, or into the stacks to get research material to complete a project, or just take a short walk around holding hands. When we'd go to the language lab, we'd try to get there when it wasn't too busy so we could sit side by side to listen with our earphones to the latest language lesson, his in German, mine in French.

It took some determination, but we disciplined ourselves to actually study, because we didn't want to lose our scholarships or flunk out.

Where's the Beef?

We also began to be disciplined about food together. While we were dating in college, one of our church members happened to have a job in a meat factory. When he spoke about being a vegetarian, his reasons helped us to realize why he had chosen that course. Some of the "horror stories" of the business had us gagging, too. The knowledge this church member shared wasn't wasted on us. Many Seventh-day Adventists are vegetarians, but not all are as it is certainly not a requirement. However, because one of the main principles of our church is maintaining optimal health, vegetarianism was in keeping with our beliefs. The principle of our bodies' being the temple of the Holy Spirit mentioned in 1 Corinthians 6 verses 19–20 is one we take seriously, and as a result it has been on record that Seventh-day Adventists on average live ten years longer than the general public. Sometimes Ben would tease when Larry or I would try an extra dessert. He'd say, "Better watch how you're taking care of God's neighborhood!"

Once Ben and I had learned that eating meat might not be good for us or for animals, we read on the subject in between keeping up with class work, and tried the vegetarian route. It was somewhat difficult to keep at this new endeavor with the menus on the school meal plan to which all boarding students had to subscribe. Although vegetarianism wasn't unheard of, it certainly hadn't attained the popularity it has now, and the offerings for vegetarians were meager to say the least.

With the little spending money I had, I would go to health food stores for protein supplements, because that's the common challenge vegetarians face: maintaining a balanced diet with enough protein from nonmeat sources. With some creativity we were able to stick with that diet, even on a campus without many offerings. We felt healthier.

We were even disciplined when it came to sweets. Near the campus on our end there was a Dunkin' Donuts. One evening after studying for several hours in the library, as we passed by we thought, why not give it a try? It was like Lay's potato chips. Although we kept going back, it was not very often, linked to our budgets but with some restraint. It was such a treat to get a couple of feather-light, melt-in-your-mouth treats to break up the monotony of studying. It wasn't the healthiest snack, but it was definitely something to look forward to. And we partook of these little delights in moderation.

In the summers, near where Ben's mother stayed in Holly, Michigan, there was a local farm vendor who had fresh-pressed cider. Oh, the full-bodied taste of that cider! And of course to go with it, they had donuts. So our donut tradition carried on in the summers and beyond. And the fact that we were "sweet on each other" didn't hurt.

These days we don't do donuts much because we are trying to keep our weight down due to the age-old "Battle of the Bulge" phenomenon. But not long ago, I discovered these new little machines that make donut holes. When you can control the ingredients to make those little temptations as healthy as possible and still have the great flavor, it's worth it. And chocolate-filled cinnamon applesauce donut holes are now a new family treat. See the end of the chapter for the recipe of this family favorite.

Looking Ahead

As Ben's final semester moved on, all the seniors began to think even more seriously about the future. Knowing the competition was stiff to attend med school, these students would really apply themselves to their studies so they could maximize their choices to have their pick of medical schools to attend. A lot of angst was floating around the campus after Christmas break, because most seniors had sent their applications in, but most had not received responses yet. Conversation over meals was intense with "Have you heard yet?" queries and the typical response: "No, have you?" I had another reason to truly admire my guy when he was cool and completely at ease, unlike the rest of his classmates. He met the query with this statement of confidence: "I'm going to the University of Michigan for med school." Of course the incredulous follow-up questions flowed: "How could you hear so quickly?" "What do you mean?" "But how can that be? You haven't even applied yet!" His calm response was "My Father owns it."

Now you have to realize that at Yale, many of the students come from families where the breadwinners are CEOs of Fortune 500 companies and the like, but to have a parent who owned the University of Michigan was quite impressive. However, what Ben meant when he said "Father" was his Heavenly Father, whom he had adopted as his own when his earthly father deserted the family years ago. When you have a Father who "owns the world," why shouldn't you be confident?

When Ben's acceptance letter from the University of Michigan arrived it was anticlimactic, because he already felt at peace about going. With that step settled, his remaining months of undergraduate life were easygoing. The coursework was more routine by now than challenging, and he had arranged things so that his final courses weren't too time-consuming. This was great in that it left him with more time on his hands, not so great when as a sophomore I had more work. But he'd assist me if I got stumped and his shared study strategies helped me as well. The use of mnemonic devices to memorize things quickly was one that I still fondly recall. And we still got to spend time together.

Graduation

When Ben's graduation was upon us, the separation that was soon to come was overshadowed by the fact that we had the opportunity to walk around the campus hand in hand and reminisce about our experiences there. I had been allowed to stay after most underclassmen had left campus, because the concert band that would provide music for the ceremony needed musicians for the program. Boy, was I ever glad I took my mom up on her offer many years before when I was ten and she asked, "If I get you a flute, will you play it?" I had played in the Yale Precision Marching Band my freshman year, and had a ball going to all the games, wearing our signature uniforms of blue blazers, white shirts, and gray slacks. So I didn't even need to reaudition for the graduation concert band.

The best thing about playing on the platform with the band was I could get a good photo of Ben marching up with his group. There was a banner carrier leading each residential college from the street through the legendary Phelps Gate, as well as banner carriers for each of the graduate schools as they made their way to their assigned sections of white wooden folding chairs. During the main ceremony on Old Campus, all the graduates of each discipline in turn would stand together for the president to announce they had made it. The undergraduates stood in groups according to their disciplines, too, and received the president's proclamation. Honorary degree recipients, of course, had a bit more fanfare. And with a hymn and a prayer at each end of the ceremony, everyone dispersed to their residential college or graduate school to receive their actual diplomas.

This was a formal yet informal celebration in the much cozier atmosphere of the residential college. We sat on folding chairs again, set in the grassy common area in the center of the dorm, and the dean of the residential college presided over the ceremony. The blood, sweat, and tears over the years were all worth this day. I rejoiced for Ben's accomplishment, and as he walked up to receive his diploma I was filled with emotion. My thought was I was the luckiest girl to be dating him and was so thankful that we had met. But luck had nothing to do with it. God had blessed us both with each other, and the "boring" year had turned out to be one of the best in my life so far.

Recipe for Cinnamon Applesauce Donut Holes

For use with the Babycakes machine

YIELD: APPROXIMATELY 36

1¼ cups white whole wheat flour
½ cup plus 1 tablespoon honey
1 tablespoon baking powder
1 teaspoon cinnamon
½ teaspoon ginger
¼ teaspoon nutmeg
½ cup (organic) applesauce (1 single serve container
   from a packet of 6 or 8)
1 egg
¼ cup vegetable oil (safflower or coconut)

Preheat the machine as you mix all the ingredients well in a medium-size bowl. Fill each reservoir of the bottom half of the Babycakes machine with about 1 tablespoon of batter. Close the cake maker and bake 4–5 minutes until a toothpick inserted into the donut holes comes out clean. Gently lift out the baked holes with the fork provided, setting them on a plate to cool, and continue until the batter is gone.

For chocolate-filled donut holes, allow the donuts to cool. Use a clean (washed and dried) birthday candle to make an impression in the donut at least halfway through, using a back-and-forth twisting motion. Fill the impression with Hershey's chocolate syrup and set it hole side up so it doesn't flow back out, until it sets.

Chapter 3

From Long Distance to Marriage

After graduation, Ben tied up loose ends pretty quickly. He didn't have a lot of "baggage," and what he did have easily fit into his car. He liked to drive and was excited to set off on his road trip to the University of Michigan. I was happy for him, but it was hard to see him go.

After he left, we each wrote a letter to the other every day, sharing interesting tidbits from classes, news about friends, and any other points that might be of interest. Monday was the best day of the week, because we'd each receive two letters, since the postal service doesn't deliver on Sundays.

We would call on the weekends when there was a little more time in the schedule away from studies. One such call started about eleven p.m., because that was the time when the long-distance rates would drop. We chatted and chatted about this and that, nothing in particular, just sharing observations and experiences. Neither one of us wanted to hang up, so we continued to talk, and before we realized it, we had talked for six hours on the phone!

We dreaded the consequences, thinking, "Oh, this is going to be some humongous bill!" The worry and fretting lasted for a few weeks, but the call didn't show up on the bill. So we waited for the next one, and the next. The charge for that six-hour call never showed on the statement. We finally concluded that the people at the phone company must have thought it was a mistake and dismissed the idea as such. What a blessing! We didn't push our luck, though. We never stayed on the phone that long again.

Sole Campus Living

Life without Ben was not nearly as fun, because it was like living without my soul mate, my other half, but I did have more time to devote to studies in my junior and senior years. I had changed my major to music and psychology and with more time on my hands, I could practice my parts more for the orchestra and the Bach Society, a small string ensemble. When I had the time, I sometimes earned a little extra cash playing in musicals put on by some of the other residential colleges. With my new musical pursuits it was almost like it was in high school, where I would play in four or five orchestras at once. I had rehearsals at least once a week for each one and would have to practice the music for each group on my own time, and in between go to class and complete my assignments. I was busy, but the busyness was a blessing and kept me from missing Ben so much.

During my senior year, my roommates and I got first pick on housing, to our extreme delight. We chose the most elaborate suite of the entire residential college, which had five bedrooms and a living room—a palace for college students. And of the five, my number out of the hat was one! So with first pick, I moved into the largest bedroom I had ever had, complete with a fireplace *and* a walk-in closet. Because my suite mates didn't particularly like classical music, I figured I could practice in the closet and it wouldn't bother anyone. There was plenty of room for it. I had moved my chest of drawers in there and could place the music on top of it, so I didn't even need a music stand. This was the best of all worlds, I thought. That is, until I overheard someone in our dining hall talking over lunch about how difficult it was to study because someone through the wall was always playing the violin. Most times after that I used the practice rooms in the music building near the center of campus. They were not as convenient, but I didn't want to prevent a fellow student from being able to study in his own room.

Along with my musical pursuits, the Yale Christian Fellowship kept me going. There were daily meetings where students worshipped and had the opportunity to interact with other like-minded students. Because of the fellowship's encouragement, the two years passed faster than I could have imagined, and I deeply enjoyed them despite Ben's absence.

Ben's Life in Ann Arbor

I was only able to visit Ben twice during those final two years of college. The separation wasn't easy, but I was assured that he was doing well. Ben and Curtis were both students then at the University of Michigan—Ben studying medicine and Curtis studying mechanical engineering—so they shared an apartment in Ann Arbor. The two studied together, and Curt said he had never seen anyone so dedicated to his studies as Ben was. He doesn't even recall Ben taking any breaks.

Like me, Ben was heavily involved in Christian fellowship during those two years. Ben's church in Ann Arbor was not far from the university, but there was no public transportation from the campus to the church, so Ben voluntarily became a "taxi driver." He would pick up undergrads and grad students from their dorms on the Sabbath so they could all worship on the day of rest. When I visited him, I was pleasantly surprised by the intriguing perspectives presented in Bible discussions during their Sabbath school. And I realized that before long his church family there would be mine, too.

The Wedding

I really wish I could tell a flowery story of a perfect romantic proposal, Ben down on one knee with flowers and proclamations, but the truth of the matter is that it was simply understood between us that we would get married. No special fanfare or poetic speeches on a particular day, but a quiet and confident mutual commitment. As Ben was nearing the end of his college career, he had prayed to God to "let the next relationship be the right one." And then I had come along, and the rest was history.

We scheduled the wedding for the summer after I graduated from Yale. We would marry at Ben's church in Ann Arbor and would have a simple ceremony. There wasn't a lot of money, so we didn't splurge, though we did have a large wedding party. Because my family is bigger, I had a few more attendants than Ben, who was kind enough to allow my relatives to stand up with him, instead of insisting on having his buddies. His brother was his best man, and my two brothers, my uncle, and my stepbrother were his other groomsmen. I had my sister and four girlfriends as bridesmaids.

Even though the wedding budget was very tight, the help of my Christian sisters made our day really special. The ladies decorated the sanctuary of the church with flowers and ribbons on the pews, and they managed the entire reception for us. My sister took care of the cake, and Ben's mom, who was really great on a sewing machine, made my lacy satin dress and veil. I found affordable fabric for the pastel bridesmaids' dresses and matching wide-brim hats that fit into my rainbow pastel color scheme. And I even found tuxes in colors to match the dresses.

A miniature accident the day before the wedding resulted in one of my fingers being in a cast. Fortunately, I could hide it in my bouquet. Everything else seemed to be right on target—until fifteen minutes before the wedding. Everyone and everything was in place to start, but the organist had not yet arrived. His mother, who was also a member of the church, explained that he was coming from out of town because he had another gig, but that he would be there. I paced the floor but couldn't calm my nerves as the clock ticked toward our start time.

Finally, about five minutes after the wedding was due to start, he came in breathless and started playing—and he played the one song I had vehemently asked him not to play. When we had rehearsed several days before, I had repeatedly requested that he not play "Here Comes the Bride" because it was so overdone in those days. Music is important to a music major, particularly on her wedding day, and I planned to get married only once! I was initially dismayed when he started playing the wrong song, but I didn't want to hold up the ceremony any longer considering so many people had interrupted their schedules and come so far to be with us. So I went on down the aisle to meet Ben—who I'm sure didn't even notice the music.

Another part of the music also ended up being a surprise. One of the soloists was a good friend from school who sang with me in the gospel choir. I had asked her to sing a special song focusing on living our lives for God. I had purposefully requested the song "All My Life," because the lyrics are like a prayer that we would "live our lives every moment all for Thee," but she had other ideas and surprised us with a different song that really didn't express our sentiments, but I guess she was more comfortable with it.

And the fact that Ben's father came was another surprise. This was the first time Ben had seen him since he was eight years old and the first time I had met Ben's father. We didn't have much interaction with him that day, but he seemed nice enough. Ben treated him cordially, but his father shared none of the words of wisdom you would imagine a father would want to impart on such an occasion.

Our minister, in a homily that turned out to be prophetic, preached to us about late nights and extensive service to others. Ben and I had discussed what life would be like with a surgeon's schedule, and I knew that there would be lots of lonely days and evenings. We knew that we would be called to make sacrifices and to offer up our lives in ways that would seem above and beyond. But we also knew that we wouldn't be without consolation; Ben knew that my music and other interests would keep me busy while he worked long hours, and we both knew that we would be together and serving the Lord, which was what really mattered. Our two years of long distance had finally come to an end, and we would face all future uncertainties together.

The Honeymoon Phase

Ben was approaching his third year in medical school when we got married. His first two years had been spent absorbing the medical school's program of study, a volume of information that some say is the equivalent of learning eight foreign languages simultaneously. He had been glued to his books and had had time to do very little but read. This year would be his first clinical year, and he would be able to actually work with patients rather than spending all of his time devouring reading material. His excitement was almost tangible as he realized that now he could put all that book knowledge into practice and actually help people medically. And some of those people might even call him "Doctor." What a feeling! Having dreamed of being a physician from the time he was eight years old, actually going onto the wards and walking the halls in a white coat was thrilling beyond words for Ben.

We lived in married student housing on the University of Michigan campus. Each building had four one-bedroom units with a combination kitchen/living room, with two units on each floor. They were relatively new and weren't big, but for a first home were quite nice, and the best part, I thought, was that they could be cleaned quickly. We were young and in love, and we didn't care how big our space was, as long as we had each other.

Ben's sense of humor is kind of quirky. I recall when we were on Yale's campus before we even knew each other, friends would say, "You two should get together. You tell the same types of corny jokes." And I remember the first joke Ben told me; it was one he had made up.

"There was a guy who was dating this girl named Kate. But

that wasn't enough for him, so he began to date another young lady named Edith. When the two young women discovered he had been two-timing them, they killed him. The moral of the story is that you can't have your Kate and Edith, too." It's a real groaner, but has elicited chuckles from some from time to time.

We laughed plenty at Ben's jokes, but we also laughed at ourselves. One evening when dinner was done and I was finishing the dishes while Ben relaxed on the sofa, he remarked on how beautiful the full moon was. "It's so bright, and it seems so close I feel like I can touch it!" I glanced out the window by the sink, noting the cloud-filled sky, and gave him a reality check. "Ben," I said, "that's not the moon. That's the streetlight!" Sure enough, the streetlight outside our housing unit was a frosted white globe on top of a tall black pole to light the way. We laughed together over that one, amazed that we never noticed it before. The thick clouds providing a solid background must have made it more noticeable. We have never forgotten how perception can lead us to the wrong conclusion, and I've appreciated how Ben is able to laugh at himself.

What we couldn't laugh at was the problem of our income. With Ben in school, we had money going out but none coming in, so I found a job at the State of Michigan Unemployment Office as a full-time clerk. The job wasn't taxing, and it wasn't long before I was one of the fastest people on the "front line," asking the qualifying questions and getting the checks run through the machines so the waiting periods wouldn't be so long for the clients.

Ben loved riding his bicycle the mile or so from married student housing to the hospital complex. He appreciated the exercise and fresh air, and he wanted to leave our one car with me so I could use it for work and errands. But a close call brought that plan to an end. One day it was still light out as he was riding along close to the curb on his way home. As he was crossing a bridge, a yellow taxicab veered toward him to run him into the railing, and then continued to try to run him off the road. Ben tried to avoid a collision, but ended up on the side of the road, with the bike down and a huge gash in his hand. We decided that riding a bike wasn't worth losing his life, so after that I would drop Ben off at the hospital for work as early as necessary before heading to work for the day.

I had fun too while Ben was working. The Ann Arbor Symphony rehearsed and performed in an auditorium that was only fifteen minutes from our place, and it was fulfilling to play with them, learning new musical works and keeping my skills up. Also, helping out in church outreach programs, preparing the lesson for our Bible study class, taking care of our first home (I even sewed curtains!), and trying new recipes were all activities that made the days pass fairly quickly.

Church Together

On weekends we went to church for worship and Bible study, and church rapidly became the central part of our life together. We served, enjoyed fellowship, and even found that our spiritual development improved our skills at our jobs. At one particular Bible study we had during this period, we were told that memorization of Bible texts sharpens the memory. We had heard before of how reading sharpens the mind as you recognize letters and form them into words and phrases that communicate concepts. The members of our class unanimously decided to test the theory, and the challenge was on. We each memorized a chapter of our own choosing over a couple of weeks and watched to see if we noticed any difference.

At the office where I worked, we had adjudicators, people who would review cases to determine the eligibility of former workers for unemployment benefits. One of my jobs was to do "look-ups." When an unemployed worker came to the office with a problem, the case would have to be reviewed by an adjudicator for a determination to be made. Due to this process, many times workers' files would not be in the file cabinets but would be on an adjudicator's desk. I had been quick on the machines, so I was elected to look up missing files. After a few times around the office checking through piles of files on these desks for various clients, it came to a point where, when I was asked to locate a specific file, I could answer, "It's on Mrs. ____'s desk, second row from the left, seven files down." It was amazing how the memory works and how I could recall such detail. I really do think the memorization helped. Ben said he noticed a big difference in his memory as well.

Aside from the Bible studies, we reveled in potlucks and game nights. Game nights were such a release. All ages were welcome. Popular board games of the time were available, such as Taboo, Sorry!, Scrabble, and Yahtzee, with Connect Four and Chinese checkers set out for the younger set. Sometimes the gents were pitted against the ladies, and you know what the result of that would be; it really wasn't fair for all of us ladies with our superior intellect to be on the same team! (Of course the men argued that their team was actually the superior one and the banter would go back and forth.)

There were plenty of opportunities for service, too. Our church asked us to teach the middle schoolers' Sabbath school class, and we thought it sounded like it might be fun. We were provided with teaching guides and came up with programs and challenges for the students to keep them actively involved in the lesson. Because we both liked games, we'd design games around the lessons and have a ball watching the kids getting engaged with them.

Like many other churches, our church has Vacation Bible School (VBS) every summer, but the first summer of our marriage, the VBS organizers were having trouble finding enough teachers for the program. They also needed a bus driver. Because pretty much all of our parishioners worked during the day, it was a real challenge. But as usual, Ben stepped up to the plate. As he had a relatively light schedule during the rotation he was on at that time, he not only learned the necessary skills by going to parking lots to practice driving the bus and got his class D license on the first try, he also picked up and dropped off VBS children during the early half of his days during the week of VBS.

At that time, I hadn't built up much vacation time at my job, but the ardent appeal for more teachers struck a chord within me. I knew it was a really long shot, but I figured, "If you don't try, you'll never know." When I asked my superior if I could take the little vacation I had in half days for a week to help out at the Vacation Bible School, I couldn't believe that she agreed. Ben and I had the opportunity to make a difference in some children's lives, *and* we got to see each other more than we would have if we hadn't volunteered and gone the extra mile to help out.

Between church, studies, work, and making new friends, our two years at Ann Arbor flew by, and soon we were on to other adventures—this time in Baltimore.

Chapter 4

Internship and Residency

Ben and I were overjoyed when he was accepted for a residency at Johns Hopkins. It was an honor and a privilege for Ben to be one of the few admitted to the prestigious institution of cutting-edge medical advancements. I was happy for him, and for me, heading to Baltimore would be another adventure. To Ben, it was a dream come true. The idea of actually working at something he'd prepared for all his life filled Ben with more than a little hope and excitement.

Packing all of our belongings in a U-Haul towed by our reliable blue Mercury Monarch, we hit the road and thoroughly enjoyed our road trip to Maryland, eagerly taking in the variegated natural beauty of our nation as it passed by. The trip went off without a hitch (pun intended), and we moved into our one-bedroom apartment on the ninth floor of the 550 Building, located just across the street from Johns Hopkins Hospital, ready for this new phase of our lives.

We knew that the internship would be challenging, but quickly learned that Ben's work there was beyond any imaginations we had. Our schedule and our living conditions were tough, although the latter was ameliorated a bit by the move to a two-bedroom apartment within the first couple of weeks.

Ben had started his Hopkins training in 1977 when a pyramid system of selection was practiced, as it was in many other medical institutions at the time. Schools would accept more MDs than slots available, and the professors would determine over the course of the two years of general surgery which candidates would be the best choices to continue their training at that hospital for all the surgical residencies. At the end of that second year, because there weren't enough slots, many went elsewhere to complete their training. Before then, these interns not only had to prove themselves to the staff physicians but were in stiff competition with one another as well. Since then, this method has been deemed cruel and inhumane, and is no longer in practice, but when we were there the competition was fierce.

Dr. Donlin Long had founded the neurosurgery department at Hopkins in 1973. By the time we arrived he had already contributed extensively to improving neurosurgical practice, and he would continue to expand the department as its chief for the next twenty-seven years. He quite capably led the department by example, with his excellent technical and research expertise. For example, he identified the glial cells of the brain and was codeveloper of the drug Decadron to treat brain swelling. He also introduced therapeutic electrical stimulation of the nervous system into clinical practice. A founding editor of two neurosurgery journals, he mentored hundreds of successful neurosurgeons not only in technique but also in their life decisions. His work with skull-base tumors, complex spinal problems, and chronic pain has had international impact, and he has been awarded five medals by international societies, while belonging to an impressive thirty-eight. Fortunately for Ben, this giant in the field recognized his talent right away, and as a mentor Dr. Long did his best to further Ben in his career.

During the first year Ben didn't get any days off. That was just the way it was back then. But did he ever learn a lot! Working with patients day in and day out, completing the necessary paperwork to ensure the best and most consistent care, taking into consideration any allergies, and keeping track of all the details was a challenge. And because the schedule was so grueling, residents learned how to do things almost in their sleep, even complex things, because there were times they would be close to that somnambulist state and still had to pull their weight.

A lunch break wasn't always an option, and often Ben would have only a few minutes to break for dinner. The hospital cafeteria did not have many vegetarian options, and at that time Ben was strictly vegetarian. Although I hadn't known how to cook when we got married, I had learned quickly. As a matter of survival, whenever we went over to someone's house and Ben raved over the food, I collected those recipes and incorporated them into our regular menu.

So at night, when Ben was close to being able to take a break, he would call me to give me a heads-up, and I would walk across the street with a covered plate in my hands. We'd meet in the cafeteria where they had a microwave, and I'd spend the five minutes watching him eat a balanced meal as he tried to talk between mouthfuls. These breaks could come at 7:00 p.m. or 11:30 p.m. or even as late as 1:00 or 2:00 a.m., but I didn't mind coming over if it would help him. He was so busy at the time that it was a treat to see him, and I knew he appreciated being able to take a break and have a solid meal to help him keep going. The area between the hospital and married housing was well lit, and I always felt safe enough to walk across Broadway at whatever hour was necessary.

Race

While I never felt my safety threatened at the hospital, we did experience some challenges with racial prejudice. For those of you who have been around a little longer than some, you may recall a movie entitled *Guess Who's Coming to Dinner*, released in 1967. It was about a young white woman who brought her fiancé, a neurosurgery resident at Johns Hopkins Medical Center, home to meet her parents. The twist on this was that he was purported to be the first black neurosurgery resident to train at this prestigious institution. Having lived my story, I know for a fact that the first black person to be admitted to that Johns Hopkins program was my husband, and the year was 1978, more than ten years after the fictitious event in the movie.

Because people weren't used to the idea of a black man in that position, you can imagine the disbelief of the general public when the subject of his job came up. Because Ben was always working, I always attended church alone, and I later found out that many of the members truly thought I was off my rocker. They thought I was crazy: first off for claiming to have a husband, and second for having one who was not only a physician but actually working and training at the esteemed and much-admired Johns Hopkins Medical Center. The minister of the church finally took it upon himself to visit Hopkins to determine if his congregation was in jeopardy with this "crazy woman" attending his church. He was relieved to be able to put his parishioners' minds at ease.

Ben's experience as the first black neurosurgery resident at Hopkins wasn't much different from mine. He was met with many startled looks upon introduction. This did not faze him, however, because he understood that people react according to what they have experienced before. None of his coworkers at the hospital had ever seen a black surgical intern or resident before. Anyone they had seen in scrubs who was black and male had always been a tech or other ancillary medical personnel. So he didn't fault them for not treating him with the respect that a doctor deserves, but was always kind and understanding when they reacted according to their previous experiences.

Dr. Long later told us that several members of the neurosurgery faculty were privately hostile toward Ben. Behind his back, they alleged that he was incompetent, but fortunately Dr. Long knew better from working with Ben:

> Just before Ben was ready to complete his Chief Residency year, the overt antagonist announced in open staff meeting that Ben was an incompetent surgeon and should not be certified as finished with his training. He stated that Ben was unable to turn a pterional craniotomy flap and expose the area of the Circle of Willis or chiasm. He indicated that he had tried to let Ben do such an operation and found that he did not know anything about the anatomy. Fortunately for Ben, I had just completed such an operation with him, in which he did the entire operation including clipping the aneurysm with minimal support from me. Nevertheless, this is just an example of the kind of situation that Ben faced in those days.
>
> Racial prejudice was alive and well among a small number of neurosurgeons in the 1980s, but it was about to die,

and did so rapidly. Ben helped it die by refusing to bend his
principles on racial equality, even for his own benefit.

Dr. Long also recounts what happened when he tried to get
Ben to take advantage of a form of "affirmative action":

> At one point the NIH (National Institutes of Health)
> had minority fellowships that were available and I called
> Ben in, telling him, "Ben, we should apply for one of
> these. They will be easy to get and they will support
> your salary at a higher level than we have now." Ben
> looked at me coolly and said, "Dr. Long, that is the only
> insulting thing you ever said to me." That stands out in
> my mind as one of his most admirable characteristics.

Ben believed firmly that everyone should be treated equally. To
him that meant educating people so that they would treat him as
well as everyone else, and it also meant refusing to be treated better because of his skin color.

Commitment to Philanthropy

Even as Ben got started on the path to success, it was very important
to both of us that we not forget where we came from. We decided
early on to be committed to helping other young people get good
educations and realize their potential. Accordingly, he took the risk
of asking Dr. Long during his application process if there would be
a problem using his spare time to volunteer. Dr. Long was shocked
and later wrote me a letter about how impressed he was:

When Ben came to Johns Hopkins in the process of applying for neurosurgery training, his concerns were unique. In those days the average workweek for a neurosurgery resident was 130–140 hours. Ben wanted to know if he would have my permission to spend his "spare" time volunteering at local grade schools to try to inspire the students to be the best that they could be. He wanted to be sure I did not have any objections.

Over the years, community service replaced a desire to do research as the number one preoccupation with every resident candidate. Medical students are very smart and they figured out very quickly that people wanted to be told about their interest in community service. Every resident candidate I saw over many years professed a serious interest in community service. Ben is the only one who ever actually did anything of any consequence.

Ben's commitments were real, based upon a bedrock of principle, and a deep concern for others upon which he acted.

This was already clear to me. This was part of the reason I married him—and it was clear to his colleagues, too.

The Beach

But all philanthropical concerns had to be dealt with only when he could get a spare moment—which was not often. One of his early rotations was at the affiliated hospital complex nicknamed "The Beach" (Baltimore City Hospitals or BCH), located approximately three miles east of Johns Hopkins Medical Center. Because the "changing of the guard" was early, about six a.m., the resident families developed a schedule to pick up and drop off the residents while minimizing the loss of sleep for everyone else. Whenever a resident was going on duty, the resident's spouse would drive him or her to the Beach, drop him or her off, and pick up the resident who would be coming off duty, driving the sleepy resident coming off a shift back to the married student housing complex. The plan was pretty efficient, but it once resulted in an awkward moment.

One morning after I had dropped Ben off at the hospital, I picked up the resident going off duty and was driving him back. We hadn't gotten far before a police car approached from behind with its lights flashing. The officer seemed to be in a hurry, and because the right lane was completely empty, I stayed in the left lane with the line of cars ahead of me, figuring if he was really in a hurry, he'd want the quickest route. It didn't take him long to abort his mission and pull me over. When he came up to the window, I figured I'd better talk fast if I didn't want a ticket. "Sorry, Officer, I saw you coming and figured you were in a hurry and would want the clear lane. We just moved here from Michigan and my husband's a doctor." I then realized it might have been a mistake to say that. Maryland is below the Mason-Dixon Line, and with a white resident next to me, we appeared to be an interracial couple. I hoped if I kept apologizing he might settle with just giving me a warning. And son of a gun, he did.

Getting the Job Done

Hopkins asked a lot of residents' families, but it asked even more of the residents. There, the rule was that you worked and got the job done no matter what it took. One professor was known to ask a resident when something didn't get done, "Did you have time to go to the bathroom?" If the answer was yes, he said, "Then you had time to get this done."

Because Ben had dedication built into his persona, he had already embraced that philosophy, which so matched his own. One evening, after having worked for eighteen hours or more per day for at least a week, Ben felt a bit light-headed, and one of the nurses who noticed said, "Perhaps you should lie down." Ben immediately replied, "Oh no, I have to keep going. This patient needs this, and the one on Halstead 5 needs that," and continued with a laundry list of tasks. He couldn't stop when he had so many responsibilities to fill that night. Finally, when he started to weave as he walked, a couple of other medical personnel each took one of his arms and made him lie down on a gurney. When they took his blood pressure, it was sixty over zero. It was a wonder that he was even able to stand up. The virus he had contracted combined with a lack of sleep had weakened him so much that he was sent home for a couple of days to recuperate. This is something that rarely occurred at Hopkins, because residents *always* worked until the job was done. They never got a day off their first year. But there are limits to what a mortal body can withstand, and Ben had reached them.

Fortunately for Ben, he didn't have to complete two years of general surgery. Dr. Long was willing to add him to the neurosurgery residency program after only one year, which pleased Ben to no end. He was delighted to move on to working in the field that was his passion and was also glad to get away from blood. Many people who learn about his distaste for blood have asked him, "How can you be a surgeon and not like the sight of blood?" To which Ben responds, "Would you rather have a surgeon who *likes* the sight of blood?" Because brain surgery involves much less blood than general surgery, his new job would be much more pleasant for him.

Research Year

After five years of intense work at Johns Hopkins, we got a little reprieve. One of the requirements of a neurosurgery resident was to develop a research project, posing a neurosurgical problem and proposing methods to solve it. A resident would have two years to complete the project as a part of his training. Ben's idea for his project was one that would interface with people from the oncology department, and several other departments, in order to find a way to treat brain tumors. As he prepared for the execution of his project, while he was still doing clinical work, he would approach the specialists for advice. To a person, each and every one in answer to Ben's queries said something like, "You know, Ben, I had been thinking about something like that myself." And then they would continue with a description of the most effective procedure for completing the next stage of Ben's experiment. Each and every one! Research that was supposed to take two years' time, Ben finished in six months. And the results were so successful that Ben received an award from the department for it.

Although his work was complete, he still had six months left in that fiscal year, with nothing left to do to fulfill his commitment.

So he and his team started developing imaging projects and other procedures that could take advantage of the results they had already achieved. And not only were they making more advances, but he now had the space in his schedule to get home at five p.m. every night. For the first time in seven years, I had a husband in the evenings the way normal wives did! I think Ben really enjoyed having the opportunity to come home at a more reasonable time and not only relax, but catch up on things he hadn't been able to accomplish while he was so busy with hospital duties. He caught up with nonmedical reading, worked on the car, could watch ball games, and even joined in with my musical endeavors.

When we had arrived in Baltimore, besides working, I had busied myself with music. Our church in Baltimore had a choir for children and one for retirees, but none for our age group. But I soon found a different outlet, accompanying a Christian singing group called the Messengers. Composed of singers from several local churches, this group would travel, singing gospel music in the area as well as in other states. But the need was still felt at the church where we belonged, so another choral group was started that asked me to accompany them on piano. I began arranging for and conducting the new Bel Canto Choir as well. We sang mostly modern anthems, like "My Tribute" by Andraé Crouch and "Jesus Christ Is the Way" by Walter Hawkins. But we also did pieces from classical works like "Cast Thy Burden upon the Lord" from the oratorio *Elijah* by Felix Mendelssohn and selections from Johann Sebastian Bach's *St. Matthew Passion*. At Christmastime we usually performed excerpts from Handel's *Messiah*. After several years of residency, and the schedule was a little more sane, Ben returned to the bass section to sing his little heart out, performing one of the arias from *St. Matthew Passion*, "Gebt mir meinen Jesum wieder!," at church in the original German.

By the time Ben began his research year, music was no longer my primary focus, however, because I was working as an editorial assistant in the chemistry department and could take advantage of free tuition. I had started attending Hopkins's evening school. At first I did it for the joy of learning new things, and would enroll in whatever class suited my fancy. Then I decided that I'd better focus on a subject just in case something happened to Ben and I had to support whatever family we might have. So I was in the last couple of years of earning my master's degree in business when Ben had this bonus time off.

Up until this time, for seven years or so, Ben had always been the one to leave, and I was left alone to wave good-bye. But the shoe was on the other foot now as I left for my evening classes and he was the one waving good-bye. I'm not sure he felt the impact of being alone the way I had, being almost constantly abandoned, though I did have my Bible and music as comforts. But he did get to learn what it was like to be alone in the house in the evenings. He enjoyed solitude like he hadn't experienced in several years, but I think it also improved his understanding of what I was asked to do as a doctor's wife.

Fortunately, my classes still allowed us to have some time together, and I'm grateful that we had those months of Ben's relaxed schedule, both to spend more time together and for each of us to understand what was being asked of the other. Those months strengthened us for some hard months ahead.

New Ones

During my evening classes, I began to be concerned when I found myself falling asleep repeatedly. When I was in college, I had prided myself on my ability to stay awake in any class, no matter how dull the professor's presentation. My newfound sleepiness was troubling to me, so I decided to get checked out. When I finally got to a doctor to receive a diagnosis, the verdict was clear. Something definitely was going on, and it was serious: I was going to have a new little one!

Ben and I were both ecstatic. Early in our marriage, we had decided to wait for a child. Ben really wanted to be a part of our children's lives, especially as he was all too familiar with the lack of a father in his own life as he was growing up. Therefore, it was agreed that we would wait until his schedule wasn't so hectic to have children. After eight years, he was still putting in at least twelve- to sixteen-hour days, but he usually came home every night, so the timing was perfect. The routine checkups started, I was popping special multivitamins, the baby's growth was charted, and all was going well.

About four months down the road, imagine our reaction when we found out that not only were we going to have a baby, but there would be two of them! I was pregnant with twins. I was extremely excited and spent hours daydreaming about how wonderful it would be to have two babies for the price of one labor. I realized it would probably be pretty difficult at first, because twins require double duty, after all: double diapering, double feeding and burping, double the supplies, clothes, furniture, and all that. But two precious little ones would also mean double treasures and pleasures. The trick would be to have the camera ready to catch each or both with all of their "firsts." Would they both have their first smile at the same time, or would the smiles be seconds or minutes apart? For their first word, would they say the same word or would the words be different? And would the words be uttered the same day, hour, minute, or second? Would they giggle alike? Would they be ticklish in the same places and laugh the same way or differently?

I enjoyed wondering about their future lives and prayed that they would always be best friends.

I couldn't just daydream, though. Now that there would be two, the planning for the birth was even more intense. Because we didn't know the sexes of the babies, we chose two boy names and two girl ones, and started reconfiguring the baby room and everything else to accommodate two. Preparations were slowed when the doctor told me I would have to go on bed rest, but that didn't color our excitement. Two little sweethearts were coming. What would they look like? Ben's side of the family or mine? Would they have long fingers like me, or would they have long eyelashes like Ben?

It was only a week after going on bed rest that I woke up in the middle of the night with severe pain. I didn't know what was happening and was becoming fearful. I think Ben knew, but he was keeping quiet. He didn't want to upset me any more than I already was, because with the babies' lives in the balance, it would be best for me to be as optimistic as possible. Ben got me to the hospital and they called my obstetrician. It turned out to be premature labor, and the Lamaze classes I had been to so far really hadn't covered this.

Our obstetrician's calm demeanor wasn't giving anything away, but with her experience she knew my babies wouldn't survive. The children were just too young for their lungs to be developed. If I had gone into labor four weeks later, then they might have survived, but at sixteen weeks, they simply had not developed enough to make it. My sorrow was immense after my two little ones entered into a world where they weren't ready to survive.

The twins turned out to be a boy and a girl. Dr. Haller was so caring in the way she wrapped the babies, even though there was no life in them. It was a hard thing, to lose these dear little ones, who never even had a chance at life. They were sweet little babies, too. Perfectly formed, and even though each one weighed only about two pounds, they were cute as buttons. To this day, they are one more reason for me to continue trying to get to heaven. I'd love to see them, hold them, talk with them, and play with them, get to know their personalities and just visit and be with them.

We found out that the twins' premature birth was not considered surprising at all. I was pretty much just a statistic. I was told that 40 percent of first-time pregnancies that are multiple births end up this way, because twins are too much too soon for a first time, too much stretching too quickly for the mother's body. Maybe understanding the reason behind the tragedy should have made it easier to bear, but the fact is my dear little ones were gone, and I grieved. In the Bible it says God will give you no more than you can bear, and although I know it's true, it's still very hard sometimes to bear what He allows to occur.

Ben and I didn't speak of the twins' tragedy to each other much. When there's a lot of pain, sometimes you learn to compartmentalize it, just put it out of your mind temporarily, and that's what we did. We had commitments to keep and jobs to be done, so we continued with life. But sometimes at odd moments, their little faces would come to mind or something else would trigger their memory, and the pain would return.

We hadn't done a lot of shopping for the babies; we had planned to go the next week. We never went, so there were no cribs to remind us, no toys, no diapers, and any baby shower that might have occurred never happened. I think we prayed together more afterward, and I also think the saying that hard times bring people closer together seemed to be true in our case.

We had been through a lot in our short marriage. Much had been asked of Ben, as a medical student and as a resident. Much had been asked of me as his wife—and sometimes breadwinner. But those trials were the ones we had signed up for. We now had experienced a trial neither of us ever imagined or anticipated. It hurt us, but we grew in our love for each other and in our faith. God had been with us, and He would be with us in the next phase of our lives, too.

Chapter 5

Australia

In 1982, Ben was chief resident when Johns Hopkins opened its new Adolf Meyer Center for Psychiatry and the Neurosciences. Dr. Bryant Stokes, an old friend of Dr. Long's and the new chair of neurosurgery at a hospital in Perth, Australia, had attended the opening. He was so impressed with Ben that he approached Dr. Long afterward with a proposal: "Don, I want that Carson lad for a year in Perth." Dr. Long thought it was an excellent idea.

Ben, just thirty-one years old, was overwhelmed and surprised. And he certainly wasn't initially excited. Never in our wildest dreams had we ever thought of going to Australia. First of all if you dig a hole straight through the earth from Baltimore, that would be the continent where you'd land. Not only was the aspect of distance factoring into the equation, but I was pregnant again and had already lost my twins. The prospect of delivering a baby in an unfamiliar environment after experiencing a miscarriage did not make the trip any more appealing. Also, the obvious fact is that Ben and I are black, and we had heard the Aussies had a "whites only" policy, which did not make us jump up and down with excitement at the thought of moving there.

Well, one by one those negative factors faded into oblivion, as we discovered that the "whites only" policy had been abolished in 1968. And although flights to Australia were long, I would only be five months pregnant when we left, not far enough along to experience much more discomfort in the travel process than I would if I stayed home. It also seemed that God was pointing us in that direction, because it seemed like every time we turned around there was an Aussie saying, "G'day, mate! How ya goin'?" And every time we turned on the TV there was a show about Australia. Australians appeared to be friendly, fun people, and we ran into them so often that Ben finally said, "Lord, are you trying to tell us something?" After prayer and a change of heart, we agreed to go.

We're Going Down

We set off in mid-July 1983. We had understood that summer in the Northern Hemisphere was winter in the Southern, but it was refreshingly cool, not cold, when we got off our long flight in Australia. It was truly fun discovering firsthand all the other things we had only heard about before. We noted with fascination the way the water circled down the drain in the opposite direction from the way it does in the Northern Hemisphere. We saw for ourselves that the "White Christmas" in Australia is in reference to the white sands of the beach, not snow.

Part of the excitement of going to Australia was the fact that we could look forward to finally saving some of Ben's earnings in order to purchase a nice home when we returned. (We had been renters up until this point.) When we discovered that in the Land Down Under the 50 percent tax bracket kicks in at $35,000, which was about where we were, that dream fizzled quickly. But we quickly saw that there was a bright side. Back in the States the malpractice insurance is about $200,000 a year for neurosurgeons who haven't had any lawsuits. And the malpractice insurance for a year in Australia back then was all of $200. Since Ben was chief registrar it was paid by the hospital, like it is done in the States for their medical trainees, so we didn't benefit from that savings. But it certainly made us more cognizant of the fact that tort reform in America needs to be addressed. Because the accuser has to pay up front in the Australian (and British) systems, there are no frivolous lawsuits, and we were inspired to push for insurance reform when we returned.

Our First Home

Our first residence on Kingston Street was in a nice shady spot and had two bedrooms and a nice-size backyard. The rental houses on the street where we lived were reserved for physicians serving in the residency programs at Sir Charles Gairdner Hospital of the Queen Elizabeth II Medical Centre near Perth, Western Australia. Kingston Street was perpendicular to the hospital complex, and the proximity of a quick two-minute walk made call duty more palatable.

The only thing that was sort of a problem for me was the location of the toilet—it was outside, a scenario that is not atypical in Australia. The bath and sink were in a bathroom inside the house, but the most utilized equipment was actually out the back door in its own little structure called a "dunny." My initial thought was that it would be nice for when you have lawn parties. But being pregnant, and having to go all the time, it was a little inconvenient, especially at night, when I would need its services more than once. And remember, we were from Detroit. With a Detroit mind-set, you don't go out at night for anything, period. I knew I was probably safe, but it just felt too dangerous to go out there alone in the dark.

Ben's such a sweetheart, he would get up when I got up, and stand guard and watch out for me while I would go do my thing, every time. Well, this lasted about a week. The poor man needed his rest so he could do his job without compromising someone's health. The next weekend, we went shopping and finally found and purchased a Porta Potti, a cube-shaped portable fixture that fit on the shelf space between the tub and the sink in the bathroom. It wasn't fancy, but it worked, and saved us both a lot of sleep and anxiety.

Western Australia was such a beautiful tropical place. Next to our house were several good-size trees, including a lavender-blossomed jacaranda about twelve feet tall. Early one morning when I took out my flute to play on the porch, I noticed the music was drawing some of the vibrantly colored parrots near. They came and perched among the branches of the closest trees. I desperately wanted to run inside to get Ben, but was afraid if I stopped playing they would fly away and he was due to come out soon anyway. But alas, he didn't come out before they lost interest and left the scene.

Within a few weeks, we moved to a different house that was only two doors from the hospital. The best thing about it was that it had an indoor toilet. Simple pleasures! It had an outdoor dunny, too, but the luxury of indoor plumbing was so tremendously appreciated. I'm not sure if the hospital moved us because someone discovered my predicament and took action or not, but it was a very welcome change. This new house had beautiful plants around it as well, including a poinsettia climbing from the ground to the roof.

A Different Approach

As I settled into our house, Ben got to work at the hospital. One of the early medical cases that Ben worked on there involved a lady with an acoustic neuroma, a tumor on the auditory nerve. There were four neurosurgery professors at Sir Charles at the time, and Ben's position as chief registrar (the equivalent of chief resident in the States) placed him directly beneath them in line of command. Actually, he was the first chief registrar, because the neurosurgery department was still rather new, founded by Dr. Bryant Stokes, the neurosurgery professor who had invited Ben to come for the year.

The protocol they had developed there for this type of medical issue involved removing the entire tumor surgically, but with that method, they would be sacrificing the auditory nerve. That would mean the lady would not be able to hear postoperatively. Ben recalled watching Dr. Long, the chairman of the neurosurgery department at Johns Hopkins, perform surgery in a similar case using lasers, but in Dr. Long's case, the auditory nerve was spared. Dr. Long's was a very intricate process, and as Ben described it to his new bosses, he could tell they were thinking, "Oh, this young whippersnapper, he thinks he can do better than we can. Ha! We'll watch him fall flat on his face!" They granted Ben permission to try this newer technique, fully expecting the outcome they had envisioned.

The procedure took ten hours. It was quite slow because Ben had to remove the tumor bit by bit, taking great care not to injure the nerve. And in the end, the surgery was successful. The tumor was completely gone and that lady could still hear perfectly. She was so thrilled that when she had a baby during the next year, she named the child after the professor she thought had performed the operation—who was not Ben! That didn't bother Ben. But it impressed the professors so much that they decided to leave him in charge at Sir Charles, the public teaching hospital, while they spent their time at the private hospitals where they could earn more. So Ben was performing between three and five craniotomies every day, obtaining an enormous amount of experience in a short time, and actually at the best time in his career. Had he remained in the United States and become a staff physician there, he would have been junior faculty, the new kid on the block so to speak, and would have been allowed to do only the routine, mundane parts of surgery, leaving the more interesting, difficult parts to the senior faculty. Whereas in Australia, where he had proven himself, he had earned the opportunity to hone his skills, performing any complex surgery that came his way. Hence, he developed a lot of surgical expertise in a relatively short period of time. And due to the efficiency of the teams there, he would still be home by six p.m. most evenings!

Perth Church

The first Sabbath we were in Australia, I checked the yellow pages of the phone book to locate the closest Seventh-day Adventist church, and Perth Church was a short bus ride away. We didn't have a car yet, so the bus was the only option. Ben was already working at the hospital, but I didn't mind going alone. This was an adventure! It was nice to get my bearings and see the beautiful, exotic foliage and flowers of the surrounding neighborhoods. Others on the bus were friendly enough to nod as they got on.

Ben could not attend church because as chief registrar, he had to be available—at least by phone—pretty much 24/7, and in those days (1983) many businesses and churches in Western Australia did not have phones. However, after a bit of thought, we agreed to approach the church about allowing us to foot the bill for a phone installation there. With a phone on the premises, Ben could attend church services and other functions held there, including the game nights we loved so much.

As with all church decisions, there was some discussion, and the church committee after some deliberation did agree to allow us to have a telephone installed. On that auspicious day, one of the elders met me at the church to let the installers in, showed them the area for installation, and we oversaw the process. I couldn't help but eagerly anticipate being at church with my husband beside me!

It's always a relief and a treat to be able to worship wherever you are, and this was no different. There's such a joy of fellowship that comes from gathering together with friends who are almost as close to you as brothers and sisters, with their similar ways of thinking on the most important issues of life. As it says in the Bible, in Matthew 18:20, "where two or three are gathered together in my name," there is a blessing that comes from God's presence. And God is love (1 John 4:8 and 10), so there's a loving presence there in any such gathering.

Part of being gathered together is encouraging one another, often through sharing and sometimes through preaching. Fremantle, a port city about ten miles from Perth, was the site of Ben's first sermon in Australia. He was invited to speak at the church there and the topic he chose was Joseph, one of his favorite characters in the Old Testament. Why Joseph? Because even though Joseph was a dreamer, he always made the best of any situation. When he was cruelly sold into the horrible institution of slavery, he didn't complain, even though he had every right to; he courageously decided he would be the best slave he could be. His industrious nature was appreciated and noticed by some powerful people in Egypt, and he rose to become the manager of a captain of the guards' household. But when he was wrongly imprisoned for something he didn't do, again he didn't complain, but became the best prisoner he could be and rose from there to be second only to Pharaoh, a ruler in a foreign land.

The Australian church received Ben's message—and us—well. I don't know what we would have done without them; our own sojourn would have been much less pleasant without their fellowship. The continuity of worship with other Seventh-day Adventists made the adventure of learning about a new culture much more fun.

Music in Australia

Western Australia, like the western United States, has its own climate, culture, and ambience. Many from the East (in the United States and Australia) would say the West doesn't have as much to offer by way of culture, but it all depends on what you're looking for. And as the Bible says, "Seek and ye shall find"; if you don't look, you usually won't find anything!

Growing up in Michigan, we had a lot of musical opportunities. It was probably due to the fact that the prestigious University of Michigan has a historically excellent music program, as well as Interlochen Arts Academy, an associate organization. The graduates from these illustrious institutions would often settle down in cities not too far away from Ann Arbor, affording excellent music teachers for the general populace. So those of us who were fortunate enough to have parents who pushed us to play musical instruments had access to a wonderfully exciting and highly proficient world of notes, clefs, and broad repertoire.

Ben started on clarinet, because his brother Curtis did. The fact that they were in different grades and their band classes were at different times made it possible for them to share an instrument—the strategy of a wise mother who knew how to get the most bang for her buck. When Ben got to high school, however, there was a need for more brass players, so the band teacher, Dr. Doakes, arranged for Ben to play several brass instruments during his high school tenure: trumpet and baritone were the principal ones. Ben advanced so quickly in his musical mastery that he was offered a scholarship to Interlochen Arts Academy, quite a coup for a kid from a single-parent home in the ghetto. His band teacher, a wise and compassionate leader, encouraged Ben to turn down the scholarship, even though it would have been a big feather in his cap to have a student at Interlochen on a scholarship. He told Ben, "You are going to be a great doctor one day, and I don't want you to get distracted from your main goal. Music is great, but your primary focus should be medicine. So I am asking you to turn down the scholarship offer." A disappointed Ben, who realized at least some of the honor, status, and opportunity of such an offer, seriously considered Dr. Doakes's suggestion and came to agree with him. He decided he wouldn't let anything distract him from his main goal of becoming a physician.

I, on the other hand, played in several orchestras in high school. And one concert that we performed every year from the time I was fourteen was the oratorio *Messiah* by George Frideric Handel. The music was so compelling and inspiring, it got to the point that it just wasn't Christmas if we didn't do the *Messiah* someplace.

This was reinforced in college when the church choir Ben and I sang in began a similar tradition and I was asked to organize the instruments for the accompaniment. We put together a string ensemble each year at our church for the performances.

In Australia, there was a boys' school near us in Perth, and the year we arrived they were going to perform the *Messiah* in December. This was not the normal tradition for Aussies. The popular classical piece to do at Christmas in Western Australia was *Zadok the Priest*, also by Handel, with the chorus "God Save the King" in it. How fortunate that we happened to get there during the right year to have the opportunity to participate in a *Messiah* performance. Ben sang bass, just as he did when we were in New Haven, and I played violin. It was quite thrilling to be performing one of our favorites together again all the way on the other side of the world the way we used to do in college.

Choral Corral (Rounding Up a Choir)

Within the first few weeks of our stay in Perth, I had an opportunity to hear the ladies of the church sing hymns a cappella when there was no pianist available for the service. I couldn't believe my ears. Their tone quality, blend, harmonies, and overall quality of sound were so extremely beautiful, I couldn't help thinking, "They really should have a choir."

Soon after, I had the chance to make the suggestion. It was Perth Church's practice on some weeks to have an afternoon program on the Sabbath. For one of the programs, they had invited Ben to be the guest speaker to comment on his experiences and the reasons why we had come to Perth. In typical fashion, he got tied up in a surgical emergency, and I was stuck filling in for him. Fortunately, this time, my experience as the volunteer church corresponding secretary for our church in Baltimore came in quite handy. One function of that job was to compose local church news articles for the periodicals that are published by our denomination. One of the more recent ones I had penned was the story about Ben's move to Australia. I was able to recall enough detail from the article that the speech was a snap.

But at the end of my speech in Ben's place, I couldn't help but ask, "Why doesn't the church have a choir?" The congregation was several hundred strong, and they had a lovely organ. The voices of the people were so rich in quality that it would be a shame not to have a choral organization so all could enjoy the combined efforts of these talented parishioners.

At the end of the program, many came up to me with words of appreciation for the suggestion and asked me to conduct. That had not been my intention at all, as I really enjoy simply singing, but I agreed, and after several trips to the local library and some music arranging, we were off.

The choir was quite diverse; the youngest member was a little eight-year-old girl named Natasha, and the oldest members of the group were retirement age, into their eighties. Even Natasha's grandparents sang with us. And there were members from various countries and cultures as well: Italy, China, Fiji, South Africa, the Netherlands, you name it. Because several members played musical instruments, we also had a brass group, flute and guitar ensemble, and a string quartet.

Word of our choir got out, and we were invited to sing in several places. Nearby Fremantle was our first foray into sharing our combined musical talents. We were even honored with a request to perform at the statewide annual camp meeting, where we sang Amy Grant's "El Shaddai."

With the choir started, transposing music became a big part of my life. For a while there, I was transposing for a couple of hours a day in addition to the time I spent practicing my instruments. Ben has always been a supporter of my music, especially when I'd hear music in my head and have to stop and write it down before it disappeared into oblivion. So when he learned I had suggested to the congregation that they should have a choir, he did not even wince at the time commitment, but joined the choir and sang bass when his patient schedule would allow it. He also didn't mind sitting alone in the church when it was my turn to play the organ for our Sabbath services sometimes.

In Australia, as in America, music continued to be my driving passion, and I was glad to continue my work. I worked even harder than before, trying to build my repertoire of transposed songs before the baby arrived and needed most of my attention.

Life at Home in Australia

Before the baby was born, and while Ben had free time, we took the time to explore and acquaint ourselves with the wonders that are unique to Australia. Ben came home early, by six p.m. every day. For the first time in our married life of eight years we would have several whole evenings together in a row—before when he had come home early, I'd been away in the evenings finishing my advanced degree. Walks to the nearby University of West Australia were not uncommon, as well as trips to local attractions. It was great to be able to spend time together, just the two of us, doing something other than the necessary tasks to keep things going. This period of time together lasted a whole year, and we really enjoyed our time with each other.

With the lovely winter weather (60 degrees!) some of the walks we'd take in the early evening before the sun had set took us to a nearby pond where we could watch the black swans with their little red beaks swimming. An alternative activity we tried was watching the "telly," as they called the TV. Back in the States we hadn't had the opportunity to watch much, because time at home was so limited. But here, it was convenient and at your fingertips, and it was exotic to us.

Along with watching television, Ben and I decided to use some of our free time by going out to eat, also a relatively new experience for us. We hadn't been there long before we went to our first restaurant. Because we both love Italian food (Ben often jokes that our name should be "Carsoni"), we checked the yellow pages and found a place that would not be too far away. Once we were close, it was difficult to locate the actual building, and when we found the place, the shades were pulled, the door was locked, and we wondered if it had closed. There was a small peephole about eye level with a sliding shutter. We tried knocking and someone finally did come to the door, moving the shutter and proceeding to ask our names. (Unsolicited memories of the *Addams Family*'s impressively tall butler Lurch sprang to mind, with his stereotypical deeply intoned "You rang?") Fortunately, we had made reservations, but now our mental reservations about the place were quite strong and growing by the second. As far as we could tell, this place either had connections with the mafia or was a very, very expensive hidden restaurant that would be way beyond our budget.

The door slowly creaked open, and we were invited to follow the solemn door attendant, who seated us in a mostly empty room. By this time Ben and I were exchanging some serious looks. He leaned toward me and whispered, "Do you think we should stay? We might not be able to afford this place!" I couldn't answer right away because the waiter arrived at the table just then, and indignantly snapped the folded napkin from its home by my plate, whipped it out with a quick flick of his wrist and placed it on my lap, all while posed with his nose in the air. I should have followed Ben's lead and unfolded mine right away. My thought was, "I'm going to be washing their dishes for a long, *long* time!" The servers brought out each individual course with a flourish, as if they were doing a slow tango or some other exotic dance. Ben and I didn't have much time to talk in between or plan our exit strategy because we kept getting interrupted.

Our anxiety continued to rise, for although the food was delicious, the menu had no prices. The demeanor of the servers and the manner in which the food was served all sent warning signals to our brains—or should I say, in keeping with the neurofocus of my dear husband, to our medial hippocampus structures. Long story short, the meal was not terribly expensive, we got out of there with satiated tummies and our wallets intact, but we never went there again. Instead we frequented a few more approachable spots nearby.

Detroit Drivers on Australian Avenues

Always fond of driving, Ben and I got a car soon after arriving in Australia. We didn't need to drive it much, because we were so close to the hospital, so we were relatively inexperienced on Australian roads when we headed out to a friend's for dinner a few weeks later. It was then that we discovered just how difficult it can be to try to stay on the opposite side of the road from the way you've been driving for more than fifteen years.

As we motored along to the friend's home, things were going fine until all of a sudden we saw what looked to be a whole legion of headlights coming toward us. We were on the wrong side of the road, on a highway with a median, no less. Fortunately, they were still a few hundred yards away and Ben was able to maneuver out of this "little problem" too, taking a side road and detouring so we could continue to the house without further incident.

We experienced a different driving problem in Perth another day. Ben was on the correct side of the street, but the police had set up a speed trap at the bottom of a hill not far from the hospital. The car we used while we were there was a little tan Mitsubishi sedan, and it was very reliable. But when the police's radar equipment reported the rate at which they thought the car was speeding, Ben disagreed with them, because that car really wasn't capable of reaching the alleged speed in that short distance once the light had changed. When he explained his reasoning to the officers at the bottom of the hill, they responded that he could take the decision to court.

Fortunately, Ben was able to take time off from work to do that very thing and was appointed a court date. As he waited his turn in the packed courtroom, he started thinking, "This is a big mistake," because the judge was mercilessly slamming people right and left. No one's explanation, with or without attorney representation, was making one whit of difference in this judge's demeanor or his heavy-handed judgments. Everyone was guilty according to this judge. Ben didn't know any of their complete stories, but he figured there could possibly have been at least one innocent person there. The magistrate seemed to think differently.

When Ben was asked to stand and present his testimony as to what happened, he explained how the integrity of the radar system could be compromised by the angle at which it was being used. When there's a slope involved, and in this case the police were aiming their radar guns up a hill, he explained that "the signal of the radar system is degraded by the angle because it's not a straight shot. Therefore the radar's reading accuracy is not reliable." He continued his description of the Doppler effect for a few minutes. The judge was captivated by the detailed explanation and finally declared, "Case dismissed," much to our relief. It pays to know your science.

Aussie Animals

A love of science didn't make certain creatures of Australia any more appealing to me, however. A few weeks after our driving on the wrong side of the road incident, we picked up a friend on our way to one of my concerts. As we traveled along at the regulated speed the windshield was suddenly filled with a wide black streak. It was a six- to seven-inch-wide band of color created by a huge hairy creature sprinting quickly across the glass. Most Americans I daresay would have jumped and run for the hills; this thing was so huge! Ben had pulled the car over, because this was a unique experience for him and he didn't know what the thing was. My friend, who had seen these creatures many times before, simply said, "Oh, that's just a silly huntsman spider, they're harmless." After which Ben and I looked at each other and just shook our heads.

Unfortunately, that wasn't our only encounter with this spider. When we had moved from our original house to the new one, we still had some mail arriving at the end of the street occasionally. Every so often I'd check to make sure we hadn't missed any important correspondence. One sunny day, I took a nice leisurely walk down the street, enjoying the exercise but moving at a slow pace because of my pregnancy. When I got there, I lifted the lid and froze. There was one of those ugly, hairy, dark gray huntsman spiders sitting on top of a pile of letters!

The baby almost came then, even though I was only six months along. The top of that mailbox came down so quickly you wouldn't believe it, as I really didn't want to disturb the big fella. He was comfortable in his new home, and I suddenly felt sure we didn't need that mail anyway. I made it back to our new house quicker than I had ever done before. And I never went back. (Fortunately, most of the mail was coming to our correct address anyway.)

Our Firstborn

Before the baby came (at the appropriate time and not induced by a spider), the ladies at Perth Church gave the nicest baby shower for me. The games were quite creative and they had even crafted a special hat and apron from crepe paper for me to wear, alerting all at the party that I was a "mom to be." We didn't want for anything with the help of the church ladies and our neighbors. On loan, we actually had two prams (short for "perambulators," the Aussie terminology for our strollers), a baby bath, and a sewing machine. I used the latter to make a cloth carrier for the new baby. Because the handy carriers weren't sold at the local stores, sewing patterns for the useful pouches with straps were distributed at the birthing lessons held at the local nursing centers. I really appreciated and was a bit proud of the pouch I had made, for when the baby arrived, it was quite convenient vacuuming with our little one tucked against my chest. I think he just enjoyed the motions and the noise.

Although our American friends worried that it might be more

challenging to deliver our baby in Australia than in the States, I had great care at the local private women's hospital. I also loved Western Australia's nursing centers where new mums could get advice on child care, have their babies weighed, get diaper rash cream, et cetera, all for free and on a daily basis. At that time, the population of Australia was less than the population in the state of New York, and the government was trying to encourage families to have more children. I was happy to reap the benefits of their effort.

Our little Aussie baby was born after just eight hours of labor, and we proudly named him Murray Nedlands Carson. Ben and I agreed that he should have a special middle name, and decided that naming him after the town where we were living would guarantee that he would always have his Australian heritage with him, along with his dual citizenship.

"Murray" was selected for a couple of reasons. Eddie Murray was a hit with the Orioles, and we were avid fans of the team. And a good friend we made while in Australia, Dr. Murray Howse, was such an inspiration to us. Although he practiced medicine in nearby Fremantle, we would get together from time to time and he and his wife Judy were wonderful people. Even though he had a brain tumor and his doctors' prognosis gave him only a few months more to live, he was always quite upbeat about things. When someone would ask, "How are you doing?" he'd reply with something like "Pretty good for an old man!" (He was in his forties.) To honor and carry on that wonderful outlook on life, we named our firstborn after him.

It was really fun to hang out with little Murray. Nice long fingers (I knew we had a pianist with this one), and nice long eyelashes, too! And he was and still is a placid guy. During orchestra rehearsals he would lie quietly in his pram next to me listening to the music for the full hour and a half without a peep! His head was full of curly hair, which all the ladies at church admired as they took turns holding him.

Only six days after Murray was born, he went to his first concert. I was a first violinist in the Nedlands Symphony, and the conductor asked me to come back to play even though I had just had the baby. Ben was on duty at the hospital and couldn't come, but my mother had come for a visit, so she attended and took care of Murray near the back of the auditorium, just in case the little guy needed some "fresh air." As the instruments warmed up, Mom was standing, rocking Murray in the aisle behind the seats up top at the rear of the auditorium. When the conductor's arms went up, Murray decided he wanted to be a part of the program and started the concert all by himself by crying out. I like to think he wanted to join the orchestra from the very first.

Ben was a proud papa, and Murray took to his dad right away. Evenings at home, we would hold our little guy and watch our favorite shows and movies. And one particular movie, *Death on the Nile*, had a theme song that inspired Ben to hold Murray under the arms and dance him around. Murray didn't particularly enjoy the activity, but Ben loved the cute little pout he would wear, so he'd bounce him around during the theme when it was played just prior to commercial breaks. Murray would be smiling by the time the show returned, though.

Murray was a hit wherever we went. A little brown baby was quite the novelty in Australia. Even though Aborigines lived in Australia, for the most part they lived in the outback, away from the cities and suburbs, and darker skin was not common where we were. While I would conduct choir rehearsal, the sopranos and altos would take turns holding Murray, admiring his skin and hair. And actually one of them heard him say his first word before I did. When she told me he talked, I retorted, "Oh, he's too young for that," but the next thing I heard was "Mama," and I realized she was right. What a smart kid to choose that for his first word! He knew where his meals were coming from.

Aussie Family

Ben, Murray, and I all enjoyed spending time with our next-door neighbors, Phil and Margaret Clingan, who, along with their daughters, soon became our Australian family. Phil was an oncology resident, and he and Margaret had three adorable little girls, who adopted Murray as their little brother. They took turns holding him and pushing him in his pram when we'd go for walks.

Our families had similar interests, and their Aussie sense of humor clicked with ours. One of our favorite shared jokes centered on the name of the hospital. Sir Charles Gairdner Hospital had the nickname of "Charlie's" among the medical personnel. There was also a supermarket chain in the area called Charlie Carter's. Not long after we had moved there, Margaret was in conversation with someone who asked where her husband worked. When she responded "Charlie's," the other woman exclaimed, "Oh, I shop there all the time!" When Margaret related the tale to me, it was a chuckle we couldn't hold in.

Because our families had similar tastes, we would have "movie night" every Tuesday. We'd take turns choosing a movie to rent, and our family would go to the Clingans' place next door, because they had to put the girls to bed and keep an eye on them. Murray could fall asleep in his pram.

One weekend we all drove to the Wanneroo Lion Park. Our

families had driven in separate cars, but once we arrived, we doubled up in the Clingans' car, because that way we could share the experience better. As we drove through, the animals roamed freely, sometimes parking themselves in the middle of the road. In the main section there were lions with their cubs. It was fun to watch them play and groom themselves in their natural habitat. Ben still retained his love of animals from his childhood and was having a blast. We all were.

In another section they had emus and camels. It had become a bit warm in the car, so Phil rolled down his window about halfway. We were watching some animals in the distance in the other direction when a friendly camel must have smelled the snacks we had brought and actually got his muzzle at least halfway through Phil's open window. Instinctively he leaned away from the huge animal, while Margaret was telling him to close the window—quite a challenging maneuver, with those huge lips trying to grab on to something delicious, but Phil got it done while leaning in the opposite direction. No one was bitten, and I think the animal appreciated his reward for the friendly visit when he located the treat that Phil threw out the window to distract him.

Phil was such a jolly sort, and I understood much better why we all got along so well after posing a specific question. When I asked him how he could maintain such a positive outlook as an oncologist when so many of his patients would not be with him very long due to the complications of cancer, he said that if he could make life for them just a bit better, then he was willing to do whatever he could for them. Ben and he had exactly the same mind-set. If patients come into your medical sphere, you do whatever you can to maximize their quality of life. Phil focused on the good he could do, not the fact that he would not be able to beat the disease, but that he could help each one deal with it as best he could. This attitude resonated with Ben and me, and I would remember Phil's response in later years, reminding me that Ben was doing exactly what he was called to do when he was out for long hours.

Home Run

While our church, the hospital, friendships, and little Murray made Australia a wonderful temporary home, we missed a few things from the States. When we had first moved to Baltimore, Ben had become a die-hard Orioles fan. Unfortunately, he could never spare the time to actually go to a game. His heavy surgical schedule and the solemn responsibility of being available at a moment's notice when his patients had complications precluded that. But his ears were glued to sound systems tuned to the Orioles sports station whenever we happened to be in the car or at the apartment. And if he had to miss a portion of a game for an operation, or a consultation, as soon as it was done and he'd made sure all was "quiet on the Western front," it was "take me back to the ball game" time.

With the move to Australia, he really tried to keep up with "Baltimore's Birds," but we discovered quickly just how far to the ends of the earth we had gone. No American newspapers could be had there from the regular public news outlets, stores, news agents, you name it. The only place where you could read an American paper was at the American consulate office, and their newspapers were always at least a week old. And although the television programming was perhaps 75 percent or more American at that time, Baltimore baseball was not a hot item of interest for Aussie sports enthusiasts.

Would you believe, of all the years we lived in Baltimore, from

1977 to 1983, and 1984 to 2013, the one time they won the World Series was the year we were away in Australia? To say we were hurt does not *begin* to describe the depth of our excruciating pain. Okay, maybe I'm overdoing this just a bit, but it really hurt! Ben took the high road on this and would actually joke about it when we returned: "Maybe they should pay us to go away again so they can win."

When the time did come for us to go home, although we were excited to begin a new chapter in our lives, we were truly sad to leave our Australian family. Murray's first few months had been wonderful, and we would miss our little home. So many wonderful relationships had been established that would continue over the next few decades. Dr. Long and Dr. Stokes had been right—this trip was the right decision. Ben's honed skills would come in handy much quicker than we might have imagined. To our relief, racism had not been a big problem, though we later learned that Dr. Stokes had actually wanted us there to help improve race relations. He had told Dr. Long, "Ben Carson will integrate Western Australia." And he wasn't far off the mark. Years later, Dr. Long reported what Dr. Stokes had said after we returned: "He told me in confidence later that Ben did more to improve the attitude of Australians to the Aborigines in the West than any other event of his recollection."

We didn't know this at the time. We just knew that Ben's work in Australia was complete, and we were ready to return home.

Chapter 6

Growing Family, Growing Career

Before Ben and I traveled to Australia, Dr. Long and he had agreed that he would return to Hopkins as full-time faculty. The staff position that Dr. Long had promised was waiting when we got back, and Ben enthusiastically began his work as an attending surgeon. He had made it to the surgical staff at Johns Hopkins Medical Center. An eight-year-old's dream had finally come true, after twenty-four years of goal-oriented focus! I can't even imagine the elation and all-out joy he felt. He threw himself into the work, and the powers that be began to notice the excellent surgical skills he had developed while Down Under.

When the Johns Hopkins chief of pediatric neurosurgery elected to resign his position to go to another hospital, the vacancy could have been filled by a more experienced neurosurgeon with a big name and, as Ben puts it, "a lot of gray hair." Hopkins's other option was to hire Ben to do the job, as he had proven that he had truly developed the skills necessary for the job while overseas. And because he didn't have a big name, they wouldn't have to pay him big bucks. Dr. Long realized that Ben could handle the job, and offered it to him without conditions.

As the new director of pediatric neurosurgery, Ben encountered a lot of cases that were not covered by a current service in the hospital. As a "fixer," he determined to develop those services so that patients wouldn't have to be sent away. It took many extra hours, because he was starting from the ground up and he had to collaborate with several other departments, but all the extra efforts were worth it, as they rarely if ever need to direct patients to other hospitals now. He developed a skeletal dysplasia program, which deals with bone abnormalities; a pediatric seizure program; a craniofacial program, which involves fixing congenital defects of the face and skull; a pediatric neurooncology program, which serves children with cancer of the nervous system; and a program to address birth defects.

To keep all of this moving forward, he usually worked twelve to twenty hours a day. This was a big sacrifice for him, as well as for Murray and me, but it was worthwhile. Ben was an advocate for his patients. That's part of what the Hippocratic oath is about. And with the health care systems that are in place now, it is more challenging than ever to ensure that patients receive the best care—not due to any limitations of the technical skills of the physicians, but because of the hoops health care professionals have to jump through for their patients' coverage.

One example really brings this point home. Ben had a young patient who was a candidate for a hemispherectomy, the operation where you take out half of the brain to stop uncontrollable seizures. Often the seizures are so severe that the patient has to be sedated so he or she can breathe. Having the diseased portion of the brain surgically removed was the only possible chance for this young person to have any sort of reasonable quality of life.

Ben spoke with the health insurance company representative, who didn't have a clue about what Ben was describing. He asked for that person's supervisor, who also was clueless. At about the fifth referral up the chain, he finally spoke with someone who Ben could tell still didn't fully comprehend the situation, because their final statement was exasperatingly expressed: "Well, we'll okay it this time! But if they need another one, we're not covering it!" (There's only two halves to a brain. If the person had another hemispherectomy there would be no brain left.)

Now that Ben travels all over the country speaking, he runs into former patients all the time. It's like being back at the hospital with friends. Not long ago, after one of Ben's speaking engagements in 2015, one of his former hemispherectomy patients reintroduced himself and informed Ben that he had just finished college and was the top student in his entire class. And that was with only half a brain. This is only one of thousands of patient stories that thrill our hearts when the kids and I consider the impact of the dedicated sacrifice of their father.

The Burbs

While Ben worked, Murray and I settled into our new home in Columbia, Maryland. The city was developed by visionary Jim Rouse, who had revitalized not only Baltimore's harbor, but also was in the process of developing Sydney Harbor in Australia.

Rouse's respect for natural beauty was evidenced by the policies put in place to govern the new neighborhood where we had moved to. No lines of any type interrupted the view of the sky: power lines, telephone and media lines, even clotheslines. Neighborhoods were family-friendly, the streets meandering so that elementary school children would not have to cross streets on their walks to school. Even mailboxes were set up in groups to facilitate relationships between neighbors. There were outdoor play centers for youngsters and their parents to meet in a safe place, and Murray enjoyed the fresh air, riding in his stroller to these places and making new friends.

We'd often go to the local library to check out not only books, but toys. We'd try out a toy, and if Murray really liked it, we'd buy it as a surprise a little later after I had returned the borrowed one. At home one of his favorite pastimes was the Jolly Jumper. Fortunately for me, he didn't mind sitting in the harness that was suspended from a doorjamb and expending his energy while I did chores, like laundry, cleaning, sewing curtains, et cetera.

It was hard not to have Ben around because we had become accustomed to his coming home by six p.m. during our Australian adventure, but we didn't miss him as much as one might think in day-to-day life. There was no time to miss him; Murray as a maturing young man was providing new challenges for me as he learned to read and develop social skills, so we were busy. And we understood Ben's calling and tried to make his limited time away from the hospital as pleasant as possible.

Something Besides the Same Four Walls

It came to me shortly after we returned from Australia that when Ben would come home, he needed a diversion during his waking hours, because he lived and breathed neurosurgery for most of his day. Considering that many operations take ten, fourteen, eighteen hours or more, his mind needed to have a rest from the continuous, draining strain of medicine. Although he tried to get home in time to see Murray before he went to bed, it didn't normally work out that way. He usually came back late and needed a distraction.

So after a quick dinner, while I was still up in the kitchen clearing the table and doing the dishes, he would go downstairs to the pool table and shoot balls into pockets. At first I was a little annoyed, but I soon realized that if all your waking hours are spent in one pursuit, no matter how enjoyable or fulfilling, the days quickly merge into one another, and there's no break or relief from the intensity. I didn't want him to go to bed with visions of surgery dancing in his head, and pool seemed like a great distraction.

I resolved that once he was done with his five- to ten-minute dinner where he kept an eye on the day's TV news, I would leave the dishes soaking and get myself to the basement so we could actually have quality time together. We could discuss the day; although I tried not to ask direct questions about surgeries, I'd ask the general question "How'd your day go?" and if he wanted to elaborate, I was all ears. Because of course I was curious. I was dying to know. But my curiosity was not more important than his having an opportunity to relax and rejuvenate himself for the life-and-death pressures that were certain to come the next day. We'd converse while playing together, mostly games of eight-ball, getting in several games before we'd call it a night. My pool game improved dramatically, and we still play when the schedule permits.

Calm in the Face of Chaos

One evening after work Ben came home earlier than usual, even before I had started dinner. We were living in the 550 Building across the street from the hospital, and we both got a hankering for some fries that night. There were none in the freezer, and the grocery store was a short drive, but there was a fast-food place only a block and a half from our building.

My hero and provider set off down the block and walked across the street. There was a short line of people, so he had to wait a bit for his turn. Just as he came up to the counter and was removing his wallet from his pocket, he felt a gun in his back.

Without turning around, Ben surreptitiously slid his wallet back into his pocket and slowly stepped to the side as he turned to the gunman and said, "I think you want him," pointing to the person behind the register.

After the encounter was over, he walked away completely unscathed, totally cool, calm, and collected. We don't know if they caught the thief or not, but from what I heard on the news no one was hurt. The fact that they didn't mention Ben didn't hurt either! We were just glad he came away unharmed!

I actually asked him what went through his mind when he felt that cold metal barrel in the middle of his back, and he shrugged his shoulders and simply said, "My thought was to direct him to the right place, the person he wanted." Although Ben is from Detroit, where muggings are a common occurrence, he was never mugged there, but his calm demeanor honed in the operating room kept him calm in the face of this new experience that for most people would have been extremely frightening.

Our Son BJ

Fortunately, Ben was also cool and calm in another emotion-provoking experience, the birth of Ben Junior, our baby who came so quickly. BJ, as we call him, is one of those people who is always about getting the job done and fast. The day before he was born, we had gone to church and were inspired by hearing about a church 5K walk that was taking place the next day. We figured that because he wasn't due for another week or so, we would participate in the 1K event and would retire early in preparation for it.

Ben's mother was with us to help before and after the birth, and we were thrilled that she was visiting. As we drove home from church, her eagle-sharp eyes spotted a patch of poke salad. This is a very flavorful wild plant with tapered leaves that mixes well with collard, kale, or mustard greens. We stopped to pick a bunch and headed on home with our bounty to have some fresh, mouthwatering greens, just the way only Mother could make them. We don't recall what else we had for dinner that day, but the greens were marvelous.

Only later did we learn that poke salad has special properties. First of all, it's so potent you have to boil it twice, pouring the water off from the first boiling, starting over with fresh water for the second one. And most people don't prepare it by itself; they usually mix it with other greens, because it's a very effective laxative—a moving experience, if you will. That salad is probably what contributed to BJ's fast and furious entrance into the world.

Fortunately, between Ben's expertise, his mother's help, and my finding a clip, BJ was just fine. When we got to the hospital and the medical personnel checked us out, BJ had an Apgar score of 8 out of 10, which meant he was in pretty good shape, and I checked out fine as well. Because he was born in a nonsterile environment, they put little BJ into an isolation room, which I called his VIP room. And he didn't have to share it with anyone, because he was and still is special, as each one of our sons is.

When deciding on a name for our second son, Ben and I were not sure if we would have another one, and we wanted to be sure one of our children had his name. We'd chosen not to name our firstborn, Murray, for Ben, because we felt he'd already have the advantages of being the eldest and having dual citizenship. If he had also been named Junior, he would have had three points in his favor that might have made a younger sibling jealous. We decided that our second son, instead, would be Ben Junior.

When BJ came home from the hospital, I truly understood the saying about two being better than one. At first it was a little hectic, because Murray and BJ were less than two years apart and a little needy. But Murray didn't mind helping his little brother, and pushing him in the stroller was fun for him. He'd bring me a diaper when I needed it, or pick up a dropped pacifier, and was pretty creative in keeping himself entertained. Having two children was definitely easier and more fun than only one, and I felt privileged that I could stay home and focus on nurturing them as opposed to working for pay and constantly juggling schedules.

Our Son Rhoeyce

I so enjoyed helping our two children develop and got such a kick out of witnessing their firsts that I was delighted when Ben and I found out in early December 1986 that we were expecting another little one. Because BJ's birth had been so rapid, less than forty-five minutes from start to finish, my doctor felt I should have this labor induced in the hospital.

At this point I have to caution you ladies: please, don't let anyone ever try to convince you a Pertussin drip is easy. Talk about hard labor! Wrenching, grinding pressure with pain, it feels like the heaviest thing you can possibly imagine is grinding down on your midsection. Ben thought I was going to break his fingers when he was holding my hand during the process. The four hours it took for Rhoeyce Harrington Carson to enter the world felt more like twenty-four. So much for a speedy birth.

At first I was trying to tough it out, but I was begging for an epidural before long. It was denied by the time I asked for it, because the baby was almost there, so I suffered on. Meanwhile, during the labor period, the doctors began deferentially asking Ben for advice, but he told them he was there as a husband and father, not as a physician, and let them do their work. They did their job well and delivered our healthy little boy.

With this last pregnancy, we tried to come up with a special name to make sure this child felt as special as the other two. The name Bryce came up as a possibility, after the canyon we had visited in Utah on one of our favorite vacations. We considered Hamilton as a middle name, but, over the course of time, Bryce Hamilton evolved into Rhoeyce Harrington. Pleased with our little one and his name, we took him home for Christmas, wearing a jingle-bell–topped little green and red striped cap knitted by one of the hospital nurses.

As Ben's schedule filled up even further, the boys and I settled into a routine in our now very full home. When we would shop, Murray, who was four, liked to push the cart, and BJ and Rhoeyce were calm riders. People in the stores liked to see them coming because on the way out they would always say in unison, "Thank you nice man [or lady] for helping us. Have a nice day! Happy [whatever the next holiday was]." And when their father would come home, they were so happy to see him, they'd chime together, "Wel-come home Dad-dee, wel-come home Dad-dee," always saying it at least three times while they jumped up and down in tandem. Dad would always have a huge smile on his face.

They learned their manners fairly easily, and we were diligent with respect to obedience, in keeping with the wisdom we found in the book of Proverbs. We tried to explain things to them as soon as they could understand so they would comprehend the logic of what we asked. For example, I recall explaining to them that Mommy and Daddy were taller than they were and could see farther than they could. "When we say 'stop,' please stop immediately, because there could be a car coming or a mean animal, or something that could harm you," I told them. We reminded them also that due to the facts that Dad and Mom loved them and cared about them, we had their best interests at heart and didn't want anything bad to happen to them. They were pretty good about obeying after that.

I used to take all three boys for walks on the back paths our town had to provide safe routes for children to walk to school without crossing the roads. Usually the walks were pleasant and uneventful, but one incident nearly scared the life out of me.

One of the laws in our town of Columbia was the leash law. Anyone using the paths with a dog was supposed to have that pet on a leash. One balmy afternoon we were on a walk for fresh air with Rhoeyce in the front seat of the stroller, BJ in the rear seat, and big brother Murray pushing from behind. The slight wind ruffled leaves on the trees, and we were pointing out birds in the trees that we saw. All of a sudden we heard pounding steps and heavy panting. I remembered a recent story in the newspaper about rabid animals, and fear for the babies almost immobilized me. But all the protective mother's instincts were coming into play as I frantically attempted to come up with an escape route. Climbing one of the trees was not an option; none of them were mature enough and I would need both hands to climb and had no slings to hold the kids on my back. Running probably wouldn't work either, because I couldn't tell from the footsteps how large or quick the animal was, and I wasn't in the greatest shape, having neglected my aerobics since the last birth three months ago. There were no shelters that I could see. Even the houses were set back from the path, with brush and brambles between the path and the backyards.

Before I could ponder my choices much longer, an Irish setter burst into view, recklessly running toward us. There didn't appear to be foam around its mouth, although it was headed straight for us. In full alarm mode now, standing in front of the stroller with all the kids behind me, I began stomping my feet and yelling as loudly as I could to discourage the dog from coming any closer. To my great relief, the dog didn't pay us any attention and just rushed past us to jump in the nearby creek. Then a man who must have been the owner sauntered onto the scene, seemingly oblivious to the heart attack he had nearly caused me. I couldn't help but scold him. "Did you realize there are leash laws? My kids and I were terrified, since we didn't know if the animal approaching was rabid or not!" My heated words didn't faze this guy, who just kind of shrugged and mumbled an insincere apology.

Still quite rattled, I hurried the boys home and settled them with oatmeal cookies, something soothing but still nutritious, and vowed to write a letter to the editor of the local newspaper. I did, and it was published, but I'm not sure it had much impact. A lot of times people just do what they want to do regardless of the law. It's still up to the rest of us to try to do what we can to be good citizens and help our neighbors, though. And that's what Ben and I have tried to do.

Volunteering

From Ben's early days at Johns Hopkins, we had agreed that we wanted to serve our country by helping promote education. Once people realized that Ben Carson was the real deal, the requests for him to speak started rolling in. By 1988, he generally spoke wherever he was asked to do so, and many of the organizations were schools. Due to his rigorous operating schedule and very limited personal time, Ben's office began arranging THINK BIG talks for schoolchildren in Turner Auditorium on the medical campus as an alternative solution for the requests Ben would receive to speak at their schools, leaving more time on weekends to speak at other venues. He could take a little break from his usual work and not have to leave the premises. It was a win–win situation. Usually students were bused in and the program was presented to eight hundred children at a time. They would be scheduled according to grade levels; sometimes there would be only high school students and other times there might be only elementary school students, facilitating the level at which the presenters would talk. Ben would have various health care professionals speak about their specific jobs to give the kids an idea of what types of careers are available in a hospital, and Ben would end the program with his talk, sharing slides of what he does, and also encouraging the youths to THINK BIG. By doing this, he didn't have to interrupt his schedule for a long time period by traveling to schools to speak. This program was scheduled once or twice a month during the school year for more than twenty years.

"This work had been his priority from the beginning," Dr. Long writes. Ben hadn't been afraid to mention the need for time to volunteer early on when he applied to the neurosurgical training program, and now that he was on staff he wasn't afraid to make it known to his superior that he was devoted to work outside of his hospital duties, even as he was considered for promotion:

> When he returned, he and I had a serious talk about his appointment. Unlike most applicants, he did not really talk about salary or laboratory support, or how many secretaries he would have, or how big his office would be. Ben wanted to know if he could have time free during the week to continue his burgeoning commitments to public service. He specifically wanted to be able to visit schools and bring schoolchildren to Johns Hopkins.

His care was genuine, and I joined him in his commitment, even if it meant his own family saw less of him.

Ben and I considered his volunteering a gift from both of us to the community. He was giving up his time at work and with family, and we were giving up time with him. It wasn't easy to have him away so much, but we wanted our boys to know that giving back was one of the most important things in the world. Ben's background was inspiring and sharing his story of triumph against the odds with others was important. We also felt the boys would profit by our example.

Chapter 7

A New Home

Helping around the house was not something that happened much with Ben during his early staff years, but not because he wasn't willing. He just wasn't around much during the day, and when he came home he was totally exhausted. Most workdays were still between twelve and twenty hours. On the rare occasions when he was home and it was daylight, it was a treat.

When our oldest was almost five, on one particular weekend he was able to take off and we had so much fun . . . laying linoleum. When we bought this house we had had only one child, and now there were three, so it was time to move on. But to do so, we'd need to update the decor. The original color of the kitchen was an olive green that had been popular in the fifties but was not at all popular in the late 1980s, and the Realtor had suggested that we redo the room in neutrals. We hired someone to replace the cabinet fronts but decided to tackle the linoleum ourselves. Mind you, the size of the kitchen was only about eight feet by twelve feet, so it wasn't the most extensive job, but what a sense of accomplishment it gave us. With those peel-and-stick squares, we were in business. Hey, we were young, didn't know how to have fun yet, and this was fun for us!

After changing the kitchen and sprucing the house up with a bit of paint, we listed it with a local Realtor. People came, but no one made any offers. We tried all the little tricks, like baking bread before people came, but no one seemed inclined to buy. One couple who had planned to come and look at our home saw a for-sale sign across the street and purchased that house before even looking at ours.

In the meantime we had been looking for a larger place to accommodate the family that had grown from three to five. Any Sunday with spare time, we would go looking with the Realtor. But there was nothing that quite fit. Then one day as I was driving around after dropping Murray off at school, I saw a for-sale sign on a rather nice lot with a builder's name on it. When we checked with the builder, we discovered that they could build a Tudor-style home, the kind we were searching for. We made a down payment and construction began.

When Ben got home on days when he wasn't so exhausted, we worked with the builder to choose plumbing and lighting fixtures. And once they broke ground, I was there pretty much every day with a video camera. I would tape the progress, and Ben would watch it once he came home so he could enjoy seeing the plan come together. It really helped to keep the workers on their toes and gave them the opportunity to ask me questions, although sometimes the workers forgot to ask. For example, in a powder room, the plans showed a sink mounted diagonally between two walls. One day when I arrived I found the sink mounted directly to a wall. When I showed the plans to the construction person, he said, "Well, I had to mount it on something." I suggested that he try mounting a board diagonally across the two walls so the sink would be installed according to the plan.

After musing over it a bit, he agreed that this would work and followed the suggestion.

With the marble tiles that were to be laid, the installer was quite talkative and told me about the marble he had on his boat. Later on, when I was speaking conversationally with his boss, he told me he wanted to hire me as a detective, because the company was missing that same square footage of marble tiles from his warehouse and hadn't been able to locate them for a while. I had solved his dilemma in half an hour.

It took almost a year, but the new house was finally complete. A Tudor style of stucco over low brick walls with a stone turret, the house also had an in-law suite for Ben's mom, complete with a kiln where she could make her ceramics. Thrilled with our new home, we put the old house back on the market, because we'd taken it off while we were busy with building. The great surprise was that it sold within two weeks for more than the original asking price. Life was good. God had blessed us once again.

Slither, Slither

Once in our new home, I discovered a guest that I did not expect. When you live in the suburbs or the country, there are certain critters that come to visit whether invited or not. The house we had built in Howard County was on a lot that was part of a farm that had been subdivided. The air was fresh, there was plenty of grass, and we even had a tennis court with a basketball hoop on one end. The barbecue grill didn't get used much, but it looked happy in its position on the multilevel deck. The playground equipment we had installed kept the kids entertained quite a bit.

One day on a weekend, I entered the kitchen in the afternoon on my way to the laundry room, passing through the family area. Once my mission was accomplished, I came back through the kitchen. And there it was. A snake! It stopped me dead in my tracks.

I don't know if it noticed me, but my senses were on high alert as I observed it. First of all its location. It was near the refrigerator, but toward the center of the room. Second, it was red, and its pose appeared to be nonthreatening, but how could I know for sure? I'd never studied snakes. Third, it was only about fourteen inches long, just over a foot, so I began to relax as I realized it would probably be easy to extricate it from our home and return it to the wild.

Rational fear was there, but I also realized that I couldn't show that fear in front of the boys, and I thought that this could be an educational opportunity for them as well as give them a chance to be helpful. Going back through the family room, I slipped through the library so Mr. Snake couldn't see me and wouldn't be frightened away. Then hurrying to the boys' rooms upstairs, I said lightheartedly, "Guess what? There's a neat snake downstairs in the kitchen! Come see!," making certain that I didn't allow any fear in my voice. Quietly we descended the stairs, tiptoeing through the library and family room, and there was Mr. Snake sitting in the same elegant S shape.

The boys all thought it was nice enough, until I said calmly, "Okay, now take it out." "Not me!" "Not me!" "Not me!" each of them exclaimed fervently. I wondered if goading would work. "Don't tell me you guys are afraid of a little old snake?" That didn't work either. Fortunately, Ben got back from work just then and after greeting everyone with a hug asked, "What's up?"

"Well, there's a snake in the kitchen and none of the boys wants to take it out," I told him. Ben immediately assessed the situation, opened the closest door to the outside, got a broom and dustpan, swept the lost reptile into the tilted dustpan, and transported the surprised creature back to his natural habitat. What can I say? Problem solving is one of his strengths.

Perseverance and Its Limits

Perseverance is another one of Ben's strengths, perhaps to a fault. Ben and our attorney Roger Bennett were both born in the month of September and quickly established a tradition of celebrating their birthdays together. Part of the celebration would be at least a few holes of golf followed shortly thereafter by dinner with spouses. Early on in this tradition, before Ben had lessons or much experience with the sport, they were out on the course and Ben's golf ball quite unexpectedly ended up in a sand trap. Well, as with any other challenge, he started working on it to bring the problem to an optimal resolution. He swung the club, and the golf ball went straight up and landed right back where it had started. He then repeated the stroke, and the ball went straight up and once again landed in the same place. These attempts to extract the ball from the trap went on for several minutes. Ben was treating this task somewhat like a tumor; you keep chipping away at it (pun intended) until the process is complete and the tumor, or in this case the ball, is removed. Well, Roger quite wisely figured they might be there all day at that rate, with Ben's dogged determination. So after the fifth try, when the ball was falling straight down once again, Roger caught it before it rolled back to its original site, tossed it onto the green, and said, "Great! Let's go!"

There are limits to the results of persistence. Although much of Ben's success can be attributed to his willingness to stick to a task, there were many times in his life and career when we saw that his success came from answers to prayer, not from anything he could do. One of these times occurred when he faced a daunting medical situation while our own son was sick.

Ben was operating on a child who went into cardiac arrest in the operating room. After several attempts to resuscitate the child, they were about to give up, but Ben pleaded, "Let's go on just a little longer, please." After further efforts, they finally got a heartbeat. However, the final assessment once the surgery was complete revealed that the patient had fixed and dilated pupils, a serious condition that frequently precedes death. The OR team was rather somber. A doctor knows the spiel, but it's still really difficult to have to go to parents and explain to them that their little loved one did not fare as well as was hoped. The parents were Christians, though, and the father and Ben challenged each other to see who could pray the hardest for this formerly vibrant child. Ben walked away from the conversation with hope.

The next day when the child's pupils started reacting to light, everyone was overjoyed. The child was making a huge recovery. Everyone at the hospital was talking about how miraculous his case was, and it seemed that the prayers had been answered.

But two days later, the child began to have lung problems. It was so disheartening to have the child's life in danger again when it had seemed a miraculous recovery had occurred. After doing all that he could, Ben left the surgical floor, disappointed in the results and sad that he could not stay to keep an eye on the patient. Understandably, he also was reluctant to keep a previously arranged commitment he was scheduled to go to in Ohio the next day.

When a weary Ben drove home, as usual he didn't speak of any of his patients, but went about his normal routine and packed for the trip that he was to take in the morning. He and I went to bed and were in very deep sleep when we both woke up to a strange noise. Poor Rhoeyce was in the middle of an asthma attack. His inhaler wasn't doing much good, so he and I dressed and drove to the emergency room of the local hospital in Columbia, leaving Ben to catch a couple more hours of precious sleep before he had to board his morning flight to Ohio. Fortunately, Ben's mom was living with us at the time and was able to take care of the other two children while we were gone.

While I was dealing with Rhoeyce's asthma emergency, Ben got a call from the hospital about the child he had operated on. Word was that the boy's lungs had deteriorated to the point where they began to fail. They were down to the last segment of lungs, and Ben was asked if he could come back to comfort the family. He agreed to come. But as he made preparations to go back to Hopkins to comfort the family, he got a call from the local hospital and learned that they couldn't get Rhoeyce's asthma under control. So Ben was back on the phone again, this time on behalf of his own son, making arrangements to transfer him from the local hospital to Hopkins. By the time he was through making sure Rhoeyce was cared for, any time he had to go comfort his patient's family was gone.

Ben left home for the airport, while I cautiously followed the ambulance with Rhoeyce in it from the local hospital to Hopkins. It was killing me not to be in the medical transport vehicle with him, but I would need a car to get us home after the doctors got his asthma under control. I held my breath as I followed the ambulance through red lights, knowing the drivers in the cross traffic would not be expecting another car to be following. There were some close calls, even though I had my flashers on, but I made it safely.

Meanwhile, when Ben landed in Ohio, he immediately called the hospital to speak with and comfort the parents, but it turned out the child had rallied and his lungs were improving. Much more than relieved, Ben took care of his commitment in Ohio and returned to Hopkins later that day, first stopping by our son Rhoeyce's room to make sure he was okay, and then making his way to see the other child he'd left behind.

The boy was continuing to improve. Everyone was amazed and pleased with his progress.

The next day Ben was due to leave for California to do a site visit. While he was away, the subject of rehab came up with this same patient's family, and a couple of the physicians actually told the family that the child would not be a candidate for rehab. They said that because his system had been compromised so much, the boy would never be able to hear or see again. This was in direct conflict with Ben's philosophy, and anyone who worked with Ben knew that. One of his principal rules is never to take away the hope. The physicians' normal predictions don't always apply, especially with God in the picture. Even if you don't have any hope, don't take it away from the family. So Ben was not happy to hear that the parents were recipients of that news, and prayed even harder.

As soon as he returned from California, he headed for that floor. No one at the nurses' station or on the way to the room said anything about the patient's condition to him as he briskly walked to the patient's room. When he got there, it was difficult to contain his joy. Not only was the child awake and alert, but as Ben walked across the room, he could tell the boy could see and hear as well. This child had beat out death four times. His pupils came back from being fixed and dilated, he survived a near pulmonary death, and he could clearly see and hear! God answered prayers again! Ben knew that this recovery was no credit to him, and he was grateful that the Lord had stepped in.

This episode had ended well—both Rhoeyce and the patient were fine—but about this time we started to consider how to make sure Ben's persistence with work didn't overwhelm family life altogether. I didn't mind that he was busy, and the boys and I had our routines. They were a little older now and after homework could enjoy games. Friday nights we would all cuddle together on the couch and read a segment of a Christian adventure series or watch a nature movie.

We had also started them on musical instruments, which of course they had to practice. I had found a phenomenal string teacher, Angelo Gatto, living less than half an hour's drive away, who had the kids sight-reading music in only three months of lessons. Mr. Gatto was not only a fabulous teacher, but he founded the Maryland Youth Symphony, which he conducted for fifty years. He was in his nineties when they celebrated its fiftieth year in 2014! Because Mr. Gatto made it so the boys could play, I'd find music or compose arrangements that worked for us, and we all played together in our family quartet, the Carson 4. We even played at weddings and bank openings. We were happy and healthy, busy, and even felt a special purpose in playing, but not even all that could take the place of a father.

Chapter 8

Family Travels

Fortunately for our family, Ben actually saw the risks of not having enough downtime, and after a while wrote family time into his schedule. He knew that if he didn't, something else would fill those slots. He really wanted to know his children and for them to know him, particularly in light of his own background, where he was denied the nurture of a doting dad.

As speaking engagements became a regular way of life, with one or more long-distance ones happening a week, not counting local speeches around Baltimore, he realistically decided that the only time he would travel to speak would be on the weekends. Not only did his day job as a physician require him to perform surgeries and take care of his patients, but also he was concerned about those patients and didn't want to miss addressing any complications that might arise while he was out of town. One little nuance that he may have noticed while checking on a patient might affect the patient later during the healing process, and he took seriously his responsibility to make sure that each patient had the best quality of care available.

The speaking engagements in which he participated on the weekends were actually scheduled during what he considered "family time." Because he didn't see the family much at all during the week, weekends were all that were left. So, as a part of a speaking engagement arrangement, he required that the entire family travel with him, including his mother, who was living with us then. You can imagine the initial complaints from the kids. "Do we have to?" "Can't I visit my friend instead?" "On my birthday?" "Gee, Dad, really? Again?" And that all-encompassing "Why?" These questions came even after we had pointed out all the positives, like getting to meet new people, going to new places, and giving Dad a chance to share with others his inspiring story of coming from nowhere to success as a surgeon to help them.

Ben didn't mind our traveling, figuring as long as we were together, we could have some quality time. Card games and snacks traveled with us, of course. We had kids! So it made sense to carry some type of diversion in case we were stranded in an airport for hours. One strategy game that Ben particularly liked is called Rook. It's similar, I've been told, to bid whist. Once Ben taught the kids that game when they were probably eight, ten, and twelve, they finally came around, and we all enjoyed the trips more. Ben and the boys would sit in adjacent seats and those across the aisle, stack suitcases with his briefcase sideways on top to form a makeshift table, and play all the way up until the flight delay was over. While he and the kids were engaged in their game, his mom and I had nice chats or read our favorite books!

It was quite a win-win situation, especially as Rook is not one of my favorites. With adults, it can get rather argumentative when partners' perceptions might be that the other one is not performing well. But the boys recalled the teams were always the youngest paired with the oldest to play against the two in the middle—that is, Dad was always Rhoeyce's partner (our youngest), and Murray and BJ made up the opposing team. BJ said his father would never simply let them win, but "would always encourage us and point out areas where we could improve." Dad's focus was more about encouragement and compassion. BJ also recalled that when he and Murray started winning more often, his dad would teach them "how to win graciously . . . or at least he tried!" BJ appreciated the team-building aspect of this interplay and concluded that the basic lessons his father was teaching were, if you lose at a game, then "lose with dignity," and if you win, "win with compassion."

Now with pool, BJ said, it was different. "Dad would let me win once in a while, but only so I would keep playing so he could win more." But over the years, BJ came to excel at pool to a point where his father was really challenged by his playing, often with the tally for the night ending up in a tie, and sometimes with BJ ending up with more wins than his competitive father! (Our attorney clued us in on the phenomenon that he discovered with his children: "You know you are getting older when you have to work hard to beat them at your favorite game!")

I also recall BJ following in his father's footsteps and developing his own eye-hand coordination in a unique way. One summer at the house we lived in that was farther out in the country, we had a problem with those little pantry moths with slender wings. Before we realized how extensive their invasion was, they had moved to the upper floor where the bedrooms were, lured by the snacks the kids kept there. But BJ had learned how to shoot moths off the ceiling with a rubber band while lying in bed! That was "taking those buggers out" at a distance of seven to twelve feet—and he never seemed to miss! It made me wonder just a little about BJ's study time; in other words, if he was using that time for target practice instead of working on his homework. But he brought home good grades like his brothers, so I didn't really sweat it.

Our kids came to enjoy the time traveling together. They all had frequent flyer miles along with Ben's mom, and although they didn't relish traveling on their birthdays, something good was always "around the corner." Going back a bit, when BJ, son number two, was turning five, he really, *really* did NOT want to go to the Virgin Islands! "No way! It's my birthday! I don't want to go!" It took some convincing, but finally we drove to the airport, caught the flight, and when we landed, as we disembarked from the plane, a whole platoon of "scouts" greeted us, complete with a marching band! And the troop leader, after shaking all of our hands, leaned down to BJ to say, "And I heard it's someone's birthday today!" When BJ looked up, he saw that the troop leader was giving him a $100 bill! God gave BJ a lesson he didn't forget!

Murray wasn't nearly as adamant about not traveling on his birthday, and because I had enough notice, I once got permission from the airlines to bring cupcakes on the plane. They made sure I knew that candles could not be lit, but the whole plane sang "Happy Birthday" to Murray while we were en route to our destination! And when we got to the venue, the whole assembly there sang "Happy Birthday" as well. Murray got a double whammy that birthday.

Poor BJ also had to spend his fifteenth birthday at one of his dad's speaking engagements. This time it was at the University of Delaware's graduation, with twenty thousand people in attendance. Of course due to the numbers, it was outside in the stadium, and it was rather warm and sunny. When the governor got up to share statistics of the class, including seven sets of twins that were graduating, he also mentioned that the speaker's son was turning fifteen that day—and a whole stadium full of people sang for BJ!

Family Vacations

We didn't just travel for outreach. We started going on vacation every year after purchasing a time-share. It happened when we attended one of those meetings where you get a free this or that for coming to listen to the sales pitch. Ben figured with his workaholic mind-set it would probably be a good investment, because it would force us to actually take time off and have good quality time as a family. With the time-share exchange system it was even better, because we ended up going to Disneyland one year, Disney World several times, and to places as far away as Málaga, Spain, pairing it with a tour of Europe on the train. When we spent time in Utah, Ben and the boys enjoyed climbing the rocks for hours at the statuesque Bryce Canyon National Park, with the gorgeous Natural Bridge. The elegant natural beauty of Zion National Park wasn't lost on us either. It's one of Ben's favorite places in America. Some of his photographs of Zion we had enlarged to hang in his office at work to bring back those fond memories.

We once stayed in a suburban town near the Utah parks where there was an arcade for kids of all ages. And the arcade owner was so touched to see a black family with mannerly children that he gave the boys each a handful of tokens! So as Ben says in his talks, there are some advantages to being black in Utah!

On this particular vacation, we had gone to several national parks with fabulous views and rock formations. As we traveled one night, it had become quite dark as we were descending a steep mountain. Although the road hugged the mountainside, the edge where we were had a sheer drop, so Ben was taking extra care not to go over.

Suddenly out of the darkness a car passed us at what seemed to be close to 100 miles per hour! We were all rather weary from a long day, so Ben reasoned, "I can just follow this guy down the mountain—at a respectable distance of course—with just enough space to stop if his lights disappear over the side." (Fortunately, he didn't voice this reasoning out loud or he might have been outvoted!) So we zoomed along the curvy mountain road. I was quite awake by this time, peering into the darkness in case I could help in some way. All of a sudden, a huge cougar jumped in front of the headlights! He must have been coming down the trail at a rapid pace too, for he acrobatically attempted to avoid colliding with either car as well as to maintain his balance on the slightly sloped road next to the extremely steep mountainside. His agility was quite remarkable! I scrambled for my camera in hopes of capturing this true Kodak moment, but alas the big cat finally gained his balance and dashed off into the darkness of the night before I could take aim.

Because Ben had slammed on the brakes as soon as the cougar appeared, we were all alert and still a bit stunned by the size of the animal and the fact that we actually got to see him. It's very rare for a sighting to occur, and the kids were ecstatic! We all felt blessed to have had the opportunity to see such a graceful animal so up close and personal (from the safety of the car!).

Amusement Adventures

Disneyland was a dream come true for Ben. He and his brother had missed out on all the rides when his family would go to the local fairs as he was growing up (there was never money for such things) and had always wanted to try them out. Ben couldn't wait for the boys to grow tall enough to go on the more dramatic rides!

The first time Murray was big enough to go with him on Space Mountain was when he was just five years old, as he was tall for his age. He and Ben eagerly strapped in and headed into the dark cavernous ride with Mussorgsky's exciting *Night on Bald Mountain* playing in the background over the cleverly designed speakers that blended into the rocklike formations inside the mountain. The ride went forward first and then backward, starting slowly and then picking up speed. About halfway through, poor little Murray had had enough, and when the ride paused, he politely asked (as he had been trained!), "May I get off, please?" Mom was more proud of the fact that he asked so politely, while Dad was proud that Murray was willing to try the frightening ride!

Once the boys were all big enough, it didn't matter how much of a daredevil ride it was, Ben was all for getting on it—even more so than the boys sometimes! Even at the state fairs in Maryland, if he could get the time off, we were there. He and the boys tried the Octopus, Round Up, bumper cars, Tilt-A-Whirls, the antigravity rides with centrifugal force holding people on the walls, and, of course, roller coasters. They couldn't just ride them once, either; each had to be ridden at least twice!

I was sorry that spinning made me dizzy and that I usually could not go on the rides with them because the resulting headaches were incapacitating. I generally held all the jackets and prizes from winning basketball tosses while they had their adventures. But whenever a shorter child needed an adult to ride with them, I would be pressed into service, and I found that closing my eyes would prevent the dizziness. You do what needs to be done!

New Orleans Object Lesson

On our New Orleans vacation, we learned all about the sea and its inhabitants at the city's aquarium—and learned a few other lessons besides. Strolling the streets, we found the ambience so thick you could touch it, an atmosphere created by the ornate street lamps of the French Quarter, building façades reminiscent of the antebellum era, solo street musicians giving impromptu jazz concerts every few blocks, and the wonderful smells of Cajun cooking.

On one of our strolls we happened by a homeless man. Because we were on our way to a scheduled event, we didn't have time to stop. One of the kids asked, "Why is that man over there sitting on the street? Can we help that man?" Agreeing with the idea to help, we responded in the affirmative. Discussing it with the boys, we all decided to provide the man with a bag of groceries. That way the man wouldn't even have to shop for the food, because we would be bringing it to him. After our appointment, we made a side trip to the grocery store and returned to the site where we had last seen the man. The kids were excited as we approached the man again. How glad we all were that he was still there and hadn't moved on! But when we tried to give him the groceries, he snapped at us, saying, "I don't want that!"

A little shaken by his response, the kids had questions as we walked back to the hotel. They asked, "Why was he so mean? Why wouldn't he take the food? It was fresh out of the store, not old or anything." Ben took the opportunity to explain a lesson: there are ways to find out if people are truly in need or if they are trying to scam the system.

Intruders

We ourselves experienced the impact of someone's not following the law while we were on a trip. One time when we were returning from a vacation, we parked the car in the carport and were about to go into the house when we noticed the side door was ajar with my violin case next to it. Slowly we entered, and the upheaval we faced was clearly evidence that the house had been broken into. We had been robbed! We began to systematically check to see what might be missing, while noticing things that were out of place. I *knew* I hadn't left the ironing board up in the family room. I *knew* the videos had been stacked neatly on the shelf. There's nothing like that feeling of invasion of privacy, of your personal space, of your life! Ben called the police and the first thing they asked was if we had called from the house phone. Of course the answer was yes. We had never been robbed before and hadn't taken any classes on what to do if it happens. The officer cautioned us not to touch anything else, because the department wanted to lift as many fingerprints from the premises as possible. All the while we're thinking, "Why us, Lord?"

After taking a thorough inventory, the police who came to the house completed the report, took our phone numbers, and said they would be in touch if anything came up. And they asked us to call if we noticed anything else missing. While they were there, I'm glad I had the presence of mind to ask them why the perpetrators would take time to put up the ironing board. They replied that sometimes the thieves get comfortable when they think that the residents will be gone for a while. Often they get so relaxed that they'll use the washer and dryer, iron their clothes, watch videos, and even cook! I was intrigued by this interesting observation, that they would not be vigilant when they knew they had done wrong.

Next came the cleanup. Ever try to get that black dust the police use to pick up fingerprints off your stuff? You could probably dye shoes with it, it's so tenacious. Persistence pays off, however, and I think I only called twice to report other items we found missing. And of course the insurance company was alerted.

Then I got the call. We lived in Howard County, but this call came from the police department of Baltimore County, the next county over. How thrilled I was when I heard they had found some items that might belong to us. They set up a time for me to view the items and informed me that a police car would come by my house to pick me up for transport to their office. As a person from a ghetto, I really did not relish the idea of riding in the back of a police cruiser, especially for all the neighbors to see me. It would be embarrassing, looking like a criminal riding in the back with an officer driving. Even if it was to reclaim our lost items, which included a nice stereo, VCR, and other electronic equipment, as well as a strongbox, I wasn't sure I wanted to do that. And Ben couldn't go, he was working. (Always an excuse with that guy!) When I mentioned my concern to the officer, he reassured me that it would be a plain car, not a cruiser, and the relief I felt was huge. Growing up I had always tried to be a "good girl," doing whatever Mom and Dad asked and trying not to get into any trouble. So not riding in the back of a cruiser was a big deal for me!

When I got into the car there was another lady in the backseat, and we greeted each other. Out of opposite windows, we each watched the world go by, lost in our own thoughts as we rode for about forty minutes to the police station in the neighboring county.

The car was quiet except for the crackle of the police radio from time to time reporting suspicious or illegal activities.

We were ushered into a small room where an officer explained to us and a few others who had arrived before us that we were all victims of theft. He told us we would each have the opportunity to look over the recovered items and claim what was ours. And I guess they always have to end with "Do you understand?" We all nodded and they took me into the room first. Once we got there, the officer told me why. Evidence they had discovered conclusively revealed that our home was one of the ones this theft ring hit.

My iron was there. (Never in my wildest dreams would I imagine someone stealing something like an iron. Fortunately, I hadn't missed it much because most of our stuff is permanent press.) All of our electronic equipment was there. Even videos that we didn't know were missing were there; I recognized the titles and the handwriting! We actually got everything back that was physically stolen.

Once I had thoroughly looked everything over, and the officer prompted me to make sure I was done, he explained what had happened. Their office had received a tip about some strange goings-on in a neighborhood. Following up on that tip, some of our dedicated men in blue had to rummage through garbage behind the place where suspicious things were reported to have been happening, and they found myriad documents with Ben's and my names on them. The biggest find was our passports, important because Ben would need his soon for a trip to Germany. The strongbox they had stolen from our house had contained all those papers. The officer continued his explanation: "Most thieves when they find a locked box like that assume that it contains valuable jewelry and possibly other items that would be easy to fence." But they didn't know that I usually don't

My dad knew what a sweet tooth I had and would sometimes sneak me treats. He started calling me his Candy, and the name stuck! Here I am (*left*) with him and my sister, Cerise, a little unsure what to think of the camera.

When I was growing up, my mom was the organist at our church, and she insisted that all her children learn to play the piano and one other instrument. The gift of music has been my constant companion, and I will always cherish it dearly. When I became a mother I made sure to introduce the gift of music to my children.

Here's Ben (*second from the right*) with his older brother, Curtis, and his cousins Marilyn (*left*) and Patricia in Michigan. Curtis tells me that even from a young age, Ben had a competitive streak—when they crossed the street together, Ben would always make sure his foot hit the opposite curb first.

(*Left to right*) Me, my brother Del, and my sister, Cerise—dressed up and ready for church!

(*From left to right*) Linzy, me, Del, and Cerise. Whatever's happening here, Del is claiming that he's innocent!

This is Ben's high school graduation photo. Ben was an excellent student, and although he was teased for being a nerd for years, in his senior year he was noted by his classmates as most likely to succeed.

Ben (*third from the left*) decided to join the ROTC after his first semester in high school. Here, too, he aimed to be the best. By the time he was in the middle of his senior year, he had become the highest-ranking student ROTC officer in the city, making him the City Executive Officer of Detroit. Here he is with other officers and adviser Sgt. Harold Hunt.

Here I am with Ben and his mother, Sonya, at his graduation from the University of Michigan Medical School in 1977. I had two years left at Yale when Ben moved to Ann Arbor. It was hard to have him move away, but we wrote to each other every day and would call each other on the weekends.

Ben and I were married in 1975, the summer after I graduated from Yale. The wedding was at Ben's church in Ann Arbor. Cerise was my maid of honor, and Curtis was his best man. The two of them are shown here standing beside us with both our mothers. Ben's mother was great on the sewing machine and made my satin dress and veil!

Sonya Carson has been a huge inspiration to both Ben and me. She was one of twenty-four children, was married when she was only thirteen, and raised Ben and Curtis on her own. Despite her difficult circumstances, she received her GED in 1969, an honorary doctorate in 1986 (she is Dr. Carson, too!), and instilled her boys with a love for learning and a strong work ethic.

In July 1983, Ben and I moved to Perth, Australia, where Ben worked for a year at the Sir Charles Gairdner Hospital. I was pregnant at the time, and our first son, Murray, was born there. We enjoyed the exotic life of Australia and loved the warm, welcoming people with whom we would form many close friendships.

Music was one of the things that brought Ben and me together. At Yale, Ben asked if I would join his church choir as an organist. Even though the audition did not go well, I joined the choir as a singer—and then got to know him better. Here Ben and I are playing organ music on the piano. I play the manual parts while Ben comes in on the pedal music.

Murray Nedlands Carson, our oldest son, was born in Australia. His middle name is the name of the town in Australia where we were living at the time. He came to his first concert when he was just six days old!

Here's Cerise with the boys. Growing up, she was a great big sister, even though she wasn't older than me by much. She has been my role model and my best friend my whole life. And, of course, a wonderful aunt to the boys!

As the director of pediatric neurosurgery at Johns Hopkins, Ben worked long and difficult days. He couldn't have done it without the help of his many talented coworkers. Pictured in this photo from 1991 are (*back row, left to right*) Visiting Fellow Ukio Ikeda; office manager Audrey Jones; physician assistants Judy Gates, Carol James, Dana Foer; secretaries Juanita Foster and Shirley Simon. (*Front row, left to right*) Secretary Linda Green, Ben, research associate Mike Guarnieri, PhD.

Carol James, holding Rhoeyce in this picture, was Ben's senior physician assistant. She was a tremendous support not just to Ben but also to our whole family, so it was only natural that we asked her to be godmother to the boys. They call her Mommy Carol.

We were privileged to have Sonya move in with us while we were raising Murray, BJ, and Rhoeyce. Here's a photo of our happy family taken in 1991 in our home library. (*From left to right*) Rhoeyce, me, Sonya, Murray, Ben, and BJ.

BJ, Rhoeyce, and Murray were all blessed with musical talent, and it was a joy to play with them as a string quartet. This photo was taken after we played for a bank opening in 1998 and received a donation for the Carson Scholars Fund, the educational charity Ben and I started in 1994.

All three of our sons were married in 2011. This photo was taken at the wedding of Murray and Lerone (*third and fourth from the left*) in December. Merlynn and BJ (*far left*) were the first to get married in March and had our first grandchild on leap day of the following year! Rhoeyce and Lilianah (*right*) had their wedding in August.

Running for public office was never on Ben's bucket list, but when the people spoke up and asked him to run, Ben asked for the Lord's guidance and answered the call. For me, the decision came down to my grandchildren. How can you not do all you can to ensure these innocent ones have at least the same opportunities and freedoms that we have enjoyed? Bill Pugliano/Getty Images even wear jewelry, so they were disappointed—and boy was I glad they were! The police were, too.

They said that without those papers they wouldn't have been able to conclusively bust one of the most difficult-to-catch crime rings in the area. And we got our passports back. We didn't have to try to replace them in short order for Ben's impending trip to Germany. God is good!

When in Rome . . .

I wish I could say that those were Ben's only brushes with crime while traveling, but that's not the case. He encountered another attempted robbery on his first trip to Italy. He and one of his colleagues from Hopkins, Dr. Sumio Uematsu, had just arrived in Rome to attend and present their research findings at the First International Conference on Human Achondroplasia (dwarfs) in 1986. It was one of Ben's first international trips as an attending or staff physician. The mystique of Rome was in the air, and pickpockets were out, although that wasn't apparent right away. Ben and Sumio were crossing one of the famous squares when they were suddenly approached by four teen and preteen girls. As soon as Ben saw them, he started walking quickly away, saying "Get away! We don't want any!" Batting his arms at the girls and trying to escape didn't actually help much, though. The encounter lasted less than a minute, and Sumio was the first to realize the girls had taken all the money he had just changed into lira—several hundred dollars' worth. So Ben gallantly said, "Don't worry! I have American Express Travelers Cheques!" in typical Karl Malden style, like the old TV commercial. (I think like many of us, he had been dying for an opportunity to quote the guy in real life, probably to feel justified for having taken the time to sign all those checks!) Reaching into his jacket pocket, however, he discovered they weren't there! And his return airline ticket was gone as well. Fortunately, his passport was in his briefcase, and they couldn't get his wallet because it was too thick.

Before we got married, I made him a wallet for Christmas one time. Some of you may be familiar with the unfinished leather kits you can get from Tandy Leather Company. You can design the outside any way you like, dye it, coat it with a finish, and then lace it together. I had learned how to tool the leather to make a monogram. This wallet is thicker than a traditional wallet you purchase today, and Ben liked to keep a lot of photos and cards in his besides the cash, which made it even thicker, so it's not easy to pick out of a pocket.

The trip to the local police station didn't prove to be very fruitful. The officers there said the only way you might get anything back is to grab one of the girls and twist their arm, threatening to break it. The children are orphans, the people they have to report to are ruthless, and that's the only way to get the others to come back with your property. But the children were long gone by then.

Because Ben had travelers' checks, he was able to get them replaced. And in a weird way it was fortunate that he and Sumio were mugged because his return trip was somehow canceled, something he discovered while he was going through the process of replacing his stolen airline ticket. If he hadn't had to inquire about his return flight, he wouldn't have been able to return on the one he thought the ticket was for and might have had to stay over another day to catch the next one. That would in effect cause him to lose a full day of work, with a domino effect of creating extra work for the administrative staff rescheduling patients and extra travel expenses for families who would have to interrupt their schedules again, in some cases causing worse outcomes for patients with progressive medical challenges.

A Working Vacation

On one of these speaking trips, the sponsors requested full family participation. We were on a Caribbean cruise, which started in Florida and sailed through the Panama Canal. Ben was scheduled to talk several times in a series on board ship, and he wasn't the only one performing. By this time the boys had developed substantial musical maturity on their instruments, and the "Carson 4" string quartet was scheduled to perform a full concert one afternoon in one of the lounges.

We had schlepped our instruments on board along with all the music books, music stands, clothes, toiletries, et cetera. Fortunately, by this time, the boys were doing their own packing. Each of them would have a checklist to work from and got to be pretty good at packing. And everything lined up perfectly for the concert.

The lounge was crowded, possibly due to Ben's plug for us during one of his talks. The title of the program was "Bach to the Future," for we did mostly classical music, starting with Bach and moving to a few more modern, inspirational songs for the end. One lady came up afterward and said it was better than being in church!

Not all behavior on that trip was holy, though. Boys being boys, Rhoeyce was a teaser, and his barometer for sensing when it was time to stop hadn't developed yet. After BJ had had enough of his brother, one of Rhoeyce's shoes ended up in the ocean. Ben spent a good half hour helping them both to understand anger: how to control it and how not to provoke it.

Teachable moments like this were the fruit of these family travels together. We might miss Ben at home, but we had these trips to spend concentrated time with him. I was so pleased to see my boys flourishing under his calm guidance and instruction and thankful for the chance to relax as he taught them about life. Fortunately, he eventually had more time to spend at home.

Chapter 9

Instilling Values in Our Children

As Ben's schedule became less hectic with the addition of more help to carry the heavy workloads, he was more than willing and finally became able to spend more quality time with the family. Coming home at eight p.m. instead of eleven or after midnight, he realized that no matter how late he stayed at the hospital trying to catch up, it wouldn't happen. So he figured he'd rather not be finished and get home at eight than not be finished and get home at eleven or twelve. He always completed the critical work before leaving, but the less critical work he would leave until the next day. A dedicated father, he realized the boys would be around for only a few more years and he wanted to know them and for them to know him. So my happiness level rose as he was around for more than just the trips, and he set about helping me train the children. It was a relief to share such an awesome responsibility. The values and principles he learned from his mother and at church that were invaluable to him were ones he wanted our children to embrace as well.

Family Times

Rhoeyce recalled how fun it was when the boys were old enough the way Dad would have each of them report a new fact each night at the dinner table. Sometimes they would try to top each other's fact with one more amazing than the last! And the conversation was usually about schoolwork and how things were going in their respective classes at their learning institutions.

Teenage boys, I've been told, are easier than girls, but I wouldn't know. We usually talked things out if there were problems. And the rules had been set. Some might say it was cruel for us not to allow the kids to play contact sports, but as a neurosurgeon Ben knew from experience just how dangerous some sports were. Murray did play tennis, BJ did shot put and discus but quickly discovered he preferred managing teams, and Rhoeyce ran cross-country. So they still participated in sports.

On the weekends when the kids were in middle school and high school and their dad had time off, they could all be found on the tennis court or shooting hoops. It was during one of those times when Ben caught a ball that he experienced severe pain in his pinkie—the type of pain that necessitated a visit to the radiology department. The X-rays revealed a fracture and a small tumor that would otherwise have gone undetected. Thus, Ben had his first experience with being a patient when he underwent surgery to remove the tumor. They took a small section of bone from his elbow, using that to replace the part of his finger that had been eaten away by the tumor. It was a sobering injury. If the tumor had not been detected and had continued to grow, he probably would have lost use of that finger, making it difficult to use that hand, which would have severely affected his career. God was good again.

Courage in the Face of Danger

One other perk of having Ben around was how he taught the boys to be brave. One particular night we were all especially startled. It was late (isn't that always when things happen?), past ten p.m. We had lost power due to a storm that was raging overhead. The wind was blowing furiously, whistling loudly, and the precipitation was that hard, driving rain that can soak through clothes in seconds, as unfortunates who couldn't find shelter in time were finding out.

Ben and I were waiting it out, reading by flashlights in our room while our youngest son, Rhoeyce, who was seventeen at the time, was doing the same in his room. A loud crash followed by an increase in the storm's volume struck fear in our hearts as the storm entered our domain. Ben had received a collapsible billy club as a gift once and had been keeping it in his nightstand drawer for just such a time as this. After a terse "Stay here," he crossed the room to the door and added, "So you are safe, let me check things out." Rhoeyce reached our door at the same time and had one of his infamous swords with him, ready to slay any dragons who dared to enter. (He's a ninja at heart. He even studied Japanese and Chinese later in college.)

Listening through the bedroom door, which I'd locked at Ben's instruction, I could hear them checking rooms, windows, and doors, and stealthily walking through the hardwood-floored halls. Ben had whispered before he and Rhoeyce were completely out of earshot, "We don't know if the wind blew the doors open or if someone is inside." It took an interminable amount of time for them to search the entire house, and the complete darkness didn't help the situation.

With the wind blusterously blowing, it probably took both of them to get the double doors closed that had been forced open in the family room. From the way they were moving I think they were trying to work together, watching each other's back. The book I had been reading held no interest for me now, as I prayed and hoped they would come to no harm.

I remained near the door, straining to hear some triumphant sounds of victory. The silence was killing me as they peered through the far reaches of the house. Then, when I could almost take it no more, I could hear my two guardian warriors strolling together, joking about the little adventure they had had! "What happened?" came from my mouth as I flung the door open. "Oh, it was just the wind," Ben said. But the fact that they were both willing to brave the deepest dark, during a violent storm with unknown perils that could possibly overtake them at any moment, made them . . .

My heroes!

Friday Nights

A calmer time spent together would be Friday night. Friday nights were always a special family time, even while Ben and I were dating. Ben's mom had set a high bar, and we followed the tradition. While she was in the hospital one time, one of her visitors was a Bible Worker, a person who has a thorough knowledge of the Holy Book and helps others to understand the precepts and principles therein. Reasoning together with this visitor, absorbing the great truths of life, Sonya decided to start observing the Sabbath as God did in

Genesis: "On the seventh day God had finished his work of creation, so he rested from all his work. And God blessed the seventh day and declared it holy, because it was the day when he rested from all his work of creation" (Genesis 2:2–3 NLT). Imagining an all-powerful God resting, when He really didn't have to, and doing it as an example for mankind. The idea captured Sonya's attention. And because in the Bible it states, "the seventh day is a Sabbath day of rest dedicated to the Lord your God," so this special day that is set apart or holy became a way of life for their family. Ben and Curtis and their families still honor the Creator with His charge to set it apart.

Sonya would "open" the Sabbath, or begin the day, on Friday nights at sunset, with Bible readings and hymns and prayer. She and her boys would each select a verse to read and discuss, and favorite hymns were sung. When they closed the family service with prayer, each in turn spoke to God from their heart about any concerns they had and expressed gratitude for blessings received. Hugs were spontaneous, as each one felt the love of God. Why Friday? It was because in the Bible at the beginning in Genesis chapter one, the description of God forming the world says several times, "and the evening and the morning were the ___ day." Jewish people still observe the Sabbath day as well.

Ben and I would also read from the Bible on Friday evenings. His favorite book of the Bible was and still is Proverbs. When at age thirteen he tried to stab a schoolmate and retreated to the bathroom to pray and read the Bible for three hours after realizing the possible consequences of his actions, he found wisdom in the book of Proverbs. To this day, he still reads from that book in the morning and before closing his eyes to go to sleep. He feels it helps him to focus and gives him a sense of peace.

In medical school other students thought he was nuts for strictly observing the Sabbath. How can you *not* study every day? they asked. The volume of knowledge that a medical student has to absorb in the first two years is enormous, so it would seem that studying should indeed be done 24/7. But Ben said resting on the Sabbath would recharge him. Taking a twenty-four-hour break, following God's lead of resting one day each week, reenergized him and made him more able to focus on the difficult and challenging tasks at hand.

In his clinical years, Ben did not always have the opportunity to rest for the special twenty-four-hour period, but again, following God's lead, he helped people. Jesus made it clear that it was fine to be busy healing on the Sabbath,* so Ben felt his conscience was clear. But if he could come to one of the worship services, he did.

When the boys were little and Ben's schedule did not allow him to join us for Friday evening family time, we had meetings on our own. After we said our verses, sang, and prayed, the boys and I would cuddle on the sofa and read stories together about missionaries or adventures from the Bible. We all looked forward to the time when we could set aside all the cares of the world and focus with gratitude on the relationships God gave us—between us and Him, and with the members of the family. When Ben was able to join us more often, we enjoyed the family sessions even more.

Education and the Carson Scholars Fund

Ben and I always valued education, thanks largely to our mothers, and we did our best to teach our sons the importance of studying. But we saw the need to inspire other students to achieve. In 1994,

*Matthew 12:12; Luke 14:3 and 4.

Murray was ten, BJ, eight, and Rhoeyce was in the first grade, so all the kids were full-time students and I had a little bit of time on my hands. We had an idea and started funding it that year, even before all the details had been ironed out.

When Ben and I would visit schools from time to time, we couldn't help but notice the trophy cases. They were filled with awards honoring sporting activities, but there were few if any awards on display for high academic achievement. And then we saw a survey comparing our eighth-grade students with their equivalents from around the world in the areas of math and science. We were shocked by the results. The United States with all its resources was not number one, or number five or ten or even fifteen, either. We were number twenty-one out of twenty-two, and we barely squeaked by for that ranking. We were just above a country where students had to dodge bullets all day!

With such an alarming statistic, we felt we had to do something. After much thought, discussion, and prayer, we came up with the idea of finding some way to identify and reward the academic superstars like the sports superstars of the school systems. We figured that by putting them on a pedestal, we could ensure that their peers and others around them would view them as the true role models they are, and strive to develop themselves as well. We also felt the need should be addressed at an earlier age than in most scholar programs, because we are trying to catch the youth before they go down that irrevocable path of self-destruction.

So, starting in grade four at age nine, a student can win a Carson Scholarship for college. They must have at least a 3.75 grade point average on a 4.0 scale, and demonstrate humanitarian qualities through some type of community service or other voluntary compassionate activities. The scholarship funds are invested on their behalf until they matriculate at a four-year accredited institution of higher learning, where the funds are paid directly. They get a statement each year showing how much the funds have grown. They also receive a certificate and a medal, get to go to a regional banquet, get local press coverage, and their school gets a trophy that is just as impressive as any of the other trophies in the school case! And each subsequent year, the scholar can be re-recognized until he or she graduates from high school.

Teachers have told us that when they have a Carson scholar in their classroom, over the course of the next year the grade point average of the entire class goes up, because there's something special to aim for. That ripple effect is one of the principal bonuses of this program. The scholars we recognize are people who would do well anyway, because they are motivated already. But with the opportunity provided by the Scholars Fund to not only earn a college scholarship early on but be recognized for superior academic excellence and to consider the future comes the idea that "If she/he can do that, maybe I can, too!" Thus the peers of the awardees strive harder to be the best they can be, and you can see how we quickly come that much closer to solving the problems of the world. The cures for cancer and Alzheimer's, and the solutions to the world's other problems, will be discovered more quickly if we have a much broader base of dedicated, well-educated young people of compassion!

The second component of our Scholars Fund takes advantage of Ben's mother's brilliant idea of reading to elevate yourself. The Ben Carson Reading Room program is designed to motivate young people to develop a lifelong love of learning. According to the National Assessment of Adult Literacy, across the country right now, the dropout rate for those who begin high school is 20 to 30 percent across the board. In the cities the rate is much higher. The statistics show that about 80 percent of those students who drop out are functionally illiterate—that is, they cannot fill out a job application. The reading rooms are designed to combat that problem. Each room is decorated whimsically to draw the students in, furnished with comfortable seating with kid appeal: beanbag chairs, rocking chairs, small Adirondack seats, bouncy bungee seats, and floor pillows. The children read to earn points and turn in the points for prizes. At first they read for the prizes, but after a while they truly learn to love learning. And of course their comprehension levels go up and academic achievement rises too. They are much less likely to drop out when they learn to enjoy reading and much more likely to have and achieve their goals.

As of this publication, there are more than 130 Ben Carson Reading Rooms in seventeen states and Washington, D.C. Most are in Title I schools (federal aid schools with a high percentage of poverty) at the elementary and middle school levels. However, there are also a few high schools that have reading rooms, with the added focus of IT (information technology). More information about the participating schools can be found at carsonscholars.org.

Perseverance works. The Carson Scholars Fund started out small, with only twenty-five scholars the first year. When others captured the vision and believed in it, we built up our board with them and expanded with satellite centers, utilizing their combined intellect and expertise. As we expanded, we had various executive directors who helped the program to grow. Our current executive director, Mrs. Amy Warner, has taken us from ten states to all fifty in the time she has been with us and keeps the costs under 10 percent! We are now at more than seven thousand scholar awards and 132 Ben Carson Reading Rooms.

Unity and Working Together

Along with the value of education, Ben and I deeply value unity and wanted to communicate the importance of working together to the next generation. This brings to mind a conversation Ben and I had with Cal Ripken Jr., nicknamed "Iron Man." Cal earned that nickname when as a Baltimore Orioles shortstop, he played in the longest stretch of consecutive games by anyone in baseball history: 2,632! And played 8,243 consecutive innings! The conversation took place at Ripken Stadium in Aberdeen, Maryland, which was named after his father, Cal Senior, the famed former player, coach, and manager of the Orioles. This stadium is where the international youth league for underprivileged children Cal established holds its games. To make it even more fun for the children *and* the adults, the ball fields there are two-thirds-size replicas of several famous ones in the major leagues, including Oriole Park at Camden Yards, Wrigley Field of Chicago, and Boston's Fenway Park. There's even a full-size replica of Yankee Stadium.

Ben had enjoyed having the honor of throwing out the first pitch, and we had all moved to the glass-enclosed viewing box above the stands. Cal's brother Billy (the best second baseman by fielding percentage in the majors in 1992) was there too. All three men have a heart for children, and the conversation flowed easily. Then Cal shared some statistics with us that are quite impressive, and in keeping with his programs to help disadvantaged youths to see the big picture. He said, "More than ninety percent of corporate CEOs played team sports." And when you think about it, we all could understand how that would be possible, considering how each player does his part for the team, recognizing his teammates' strengths and weaknesses, and fills in when necessary to accomplish the goal of winning.

The next statistic was just as impactful, if not more so: "More than ninety percent of prisoners did *not* play team sports." Kinda gives you goose bumps, huh? The message these statistics render allows us to comprehend how working together just was not part of these individuals' practice in growing up. Learning how to deal with various personalities, not being envious of anyone else's talent but working with them to achieve a common goal . . . these concepts were not a part of their life experiences and therefore were not in their "life skills vocabulary." Cal's idea of providing an avenue for these deprived youth to have a better chance at success in life resonated with us deeply. If we don't support the future generations, and help them to be the best they can be, who will?

Discipline

Speaking of supporting future generations, our children weren't exempt from the need for correction. Rhoeyce recalls his father as one who really knew how to discipline. The incidents he remembered occurred in high school, when Ben's schedule had become more reasonable and he could get home a little earlier.

As Rhoeyce shared his thoughts, it was with admiration for the manner in which his father would help him understand his mistake. He said, "Dad always would fit the punishment to the crime, and it would be fair." If Rhoeyce forgot to hand in his homework, his dad would require him to write a book report or something similar. If the problem was of greater magnitude, Dad would discuss the problem with Rhoeyce prior to administering the punishment.

There was once a serious infraction he had committed, and Rhoeyce remembers his father asking questions about why he thought it happened, helping him to understand that there are consequences for our actions. The infraction in this case was crashing the car. But Rhoeyce hadn't just crashed one—he had caused damage to two cars in one month! He said his father talked with him for about half an hour about why this happened, what he was thinking, how he might have avoided the crashes, what he should do the next time, what the consequences are when you damage a car or when you don't keep your focus on driving, and how someone might get hurt or killed. They then prayed about it. Usually Rhoeyce would do almost anything to avoid a spanking. But after that talk, Rhoeyce felt worse for having done what he did than he feared the penalty he knew was about to come.

This was a different sort of disciplinary problem, not a physical one, and Ben felt it needed to be handled in a special way. Talking through the situation and helping Rhoeyce gain a full understanding of the consequences was a part of the healing process. Once Rhoeyce understood more fully that actions have consequences, he would think twice before going that route again.

Our eldest son's, Murray's, memories are even more focused on the caring, compassionate side of his father:

> It was a hot, sunny summer day, and Dad was showing me something I really wasn't interested in. A riding mower? What was I supposed to do with this thing? I was only fourteen and figured, he's going to want me to clean it, or oil it, or something. I was looking forward to spending some time with friends and didn't really pay attention, because it simply was not of interest to me. I

think it was a big deal to him because he must have seen people using them while he was growing up. Anyway, he was happy about having it because for one thing it would cut down on the time it took to cut the grass. Being the oldest, it was only natural that Dad wanted me to learn about the tractor first. Being me, it was only natural that I was reluctant. Despite my attempts to put up a show of indifference, apathy, and even a little antipathy, he persisted in teaching me about the mower.

"This is the gas," he said, pointing at the pedal. "Here's the on/off switch. . . ."

He pointed at and indicated several other controls for the machine and briefly demonstrated them. Imagine my surprise, then, when he said, "Okay, now you try it." I suppose that by my not being interested in things it made it that much more appealing to try to get me to do them, and had I known then some of what I know now I would have feigned interest in a lot more things in order to get out of doing them! Personal commentary aside, seeing as how I'd been "such an attentive student," I knew exactly how to operate the lawn mower. I got on the tractor and drove in a straight line. All was going well until the lawn ended abruptly and a large bush got in the way. Seeing as how I had "paid attention" to the instructions, I not-so-calmly leapt from the tractor moments before it plowed into the bush. Thus ended my roughly ten-second riding mower jaunt. My incredible display of athleticism was not met with the accolades I expected; instead, my dad quickly stopped the tractor from fighting with the bush and explained to me several ways I could have avoided the situation.

All kidding aside, I actually felt terrible about what I had done. I was relieved to see that while there was some sap on the tractor and a gash in the bush, it was but a flesh wound for the plant, from which it could easily recover. Looking back and thinking on the human tendency to remember the negative, the fact that the most vivid memory from that experience was seeing green goo on the plant and the tractor reminds me just how calm my dad was. He was significantly more concerned that I wasn't hurt than he was at how horribly I had failed my first "driving" test. Even after assessing my well-being he wasn't upset with me, but simply reassessed and decided that maybe it was a bit early for me. I don't recall ever really riding the riding mower and I believe my parents ended up paying to have the lawn cut—they probably didn't want to have to replace the entire garden! They never indicated that it was my fault, though. And for those who would believe I'm a bad driver now, I have never received a speeding ticket and by the grace of God I've only received one written warning.

Long story short: I didn't see my dad all the time, but I could tell when I did see him that he cared deeply for all of us.

Teaching Hard Work

Ben Junior's memories were more about personal responsibility and hard work.

When he finally got his driver's license, BJ was ready. He

wanted to cruise around, being the cool dude with the cool ride! BJ thoroughly enjoyed driving, unlike his older brother. Murray rode the bus to high school even as a senior—unthinkable for most in his position. But there was method behind his ostensible madness. His best friend, also a senior in high school, rode the bus as well, so the two would have extra time to visit in the backseat from whence they "ruled."

But BJ had no such inclinations. He had the license, he had the ride, and he had the drive to drive. His primary problem: gas. He had use of a car, and each of the boys had allowances, but BJ didn't feel it was enough for the amount of gas he needed for the things he wanted to do. So he found unique ways to make money to cover this rising commodity. He would take an early lunch and drive over to a nearby popular fast-food restaurant, returning to the campus to offer alternatives to the students during the remainder of his own lunch hour. He also would offer rides home to students who didn't want to take the bus—and would charge them. He even sold candy to the elementary students for more than it cost him. His reasoning? If they want it, they can pay for it. The convenience of having the goodies—BJ had to use his time and gas to go get them—should be worth it to those who really wanted the items.

When BJ went to college, his dad would require him to write up a college budget. This would be by semester, with cost comparisons of options and BJ's preferences for those options. He was to present a written cost and benefit analysis comparing living on campus with the alternative of living off campus, supplying a narrative summary of the qualitative elements of each option. Ben called this "presenting a business case." BJ complied with the request and believes that this encouraged the entrepreneurial spirit that has helped him make his way in the world. The other boys lived on their college campuses, but

BJ wanted to try living off campus after his freshman year. And after doing his due diligence he was able to achieve that goal.

The take-home points that he felt he should share from what his father taught him over the years were that you have to "make your own way, work for what you get because nothing is free, and always be at least twice as good at what you do as the next person."

Adult Children

Murray followed in Dad and Mom's footsteps, attending Yale, and completed his undergraduate degree in mechanical engineering like his uncle Curtis. During the writing of this book, he completed his master's in information technology. BJ has worked as a vice president with the Warner Companies and as an entrepreneur specializing in mergers and acquisitions. He founded and/or purchased his eleventh company before he reached his thirtieth birthday. Rhoeyce, meanwhile, has been a certified public accountant for a few years.

All three of our sons got married in 2011 to wonderful Christian women, and two of them gave us granddaughters, so we are now Grandpop and Mumsee! Whenever we get back to Maryland we try to see them, but it doesn't happen often, perhaps four times a year. When we do see the grandkids, it's like Christmas, watching their little antics and seeing how much they have matured since our last visit!

Ben and I are both so proud of our sons. They have grown to be responsible, Christian adults with good character and good values. We feel very blessed and thankful.

Chapter 10

Being the Doctor's Wife

Though I maintained my work, I considered my family role, being Ben's wife and the boys' mother, my main career. Before we even considered marriage, I realized that being Ben's wife was going to carry certain responsibilities. Initially, it meant supporting him through long hours of studying. Later, it meant being willing to be without him for long stretches of time. During those periods, I didn't always know much about his day-to-day life, because I'd see him for just a few minutes of each waking day. And when the boys came, I had to be the anchor, like a lot of single parents do. For many years no one else was around to do it. But the focus on the boys and their maturation in all the facets of their lives, although demanding, brought with that intense demand a sense of fulfillment and satisfaction. When you'd see them helping out someone who was not as fortunate, or befriending another child because the others were shunning him, it would fill my soul with such warmth. Yes, they had their moments, but now these young men are quite thoughtful of others, engage voluntarily in charity work, and support their families, not only monetarily but logistically and emotionally as well.

In the course of writing this book, I was musing about how busy I was with our family and began to reflect on Ben's "other family." Considering the time Ben spent at the hospital, the people who worked with him were like a family. And because he spent more time with that family than with us it seemed only fair that input from that family should be included in this book. You cannot imagine how much more thankful I have become for the people whom I already admired who worked with him. And that they were generously willing to share stories considering their extremely hectic schedules is even more humbling. It's been amazing to learn new things about the man I've loved for so many years. It's helped me to understand him more, to love him even more, and to know how best to pray for him as well.

Hearing the Call and Following Through (Thoroughly)

Many people have heard about Ben separating conjoined twins, but few have heard the full story, and even fewer have heard the testimony of his mentor, so I will share the whole tale again here. You know how people get a gut feeling? Or an urge to do something off the beaten path, out of the ordinary? We've found out that it's good to follow that urge. Case in point: In 1986, Ben developed this incredible appetite for information on craniopagus Siamese twins (those joined at the head). He couldn't read enough about them! He studied and studied to find out as much about them as he could. What he discovered in his research was that surgical attempts to separate these types of twins had an extremely high mortality rate, and hardly any survived. After studying many cases for a couple of months, Ben concluded that the primary reason they did not survive was exsanguination, or bleeding to death.

A "fixer" by nature, he brainstormed to come up with a remedy. Recalling stories of children falling through the ice and surviving even after an hour of submersion, he surmised that perhaps the same sort of process could be utilized in a clinical setting. He spoke to one of the cardiologists about the phenomenon of a child's survival in the cold, and together they came up with a plan that could work for a set of Siamese twins. By cooling the blood, the hearts would stop beating, and the blood would be circulated through special machines that would prevent clotting. With the blood out of the bodies, surgeons could see the anatomy better, and as long as they completed their operation within an hour the children would be fine—no brain damage. Then Ben thought, "Why in the world am I reading about these twins? The birth of craniopagus Siamese twins occurs only once in two million births! The chances that I'll ever see a case like this are virtually nil!"

But a few weeks later, doctors from Germany came to Johns Hopkins with the case of the Binder Siamese twins. When the mother, Theresa Binder, was told by doctors in her country that she would have to choose which twin would survive and which would have to die, she could not make that choice. Early in her pregnancy when she was told that she had an abnormal situation with her babies, she could not bring herself to abort. She even thought of killing herself, but then she realized that if she did, she would be taking three lives instead of just one, and she simply couldn't do it, because of the unfairness to the children, who had no say in the matter.

The German doctors came to Dr. Mark Rogers in the Department of Anesthesiology, inquiring about the possibility of separating the twins. Were there any new methods that had been developed? Had any new procedures been attempted? What kind of prognosis could they give?

Dr. Rogers approached Ben as the chief of pediatric neurosurgery. He knew that Ben had been involved in some cutting-edge procedures. Ben's answer to Dr. Rogers's query, "There might be a way to do this," was followed with the procedures he and the cardiologist had discussed. And so the planning began.

With any surgery, you have to have contingency plans, because most surgeries are not straightforward. There always seem to be extra tissue to deal with, abnormal arterial and venous structures, scarring, skull abnormalities, and/or other anomalous structures to complicate matters. To minimize these, planning is usually as in-depth as possible. The operating room had to be rewired to accommodate double the equipment, because in essence there would be two patients being operated on. Nurses were clever in devising special accordion-like drapes for the patients so that when the twins were separated and the tables would be pulled away from each other, the drapes would fall into place without contaminating the field.

In preparation for the surgery, Ben would close his eyes and imagine the entire surgery step by step from beginning to end, while a nurse took notes on how things would unfold. This preparation was critically important, because there would be seventy people involved in the operation, and movements had to be choreographed so that the health care professionals would not be in one another's way. (And remember, the room already would be populated with twice the equipment as usual.)

Even with all the preparation, the neurosurgeons would still be under quite a bit of pressure once the blood had been drained from the twins. In only one hour, the two teams would each have to reconstruct all the blood vessels where they were parted. Keep in mind that when the separation takes place, each child would have only half of the blood vessels at the site of the separation—like splitting a straw down the middle, the long way. And the surgeons had to reconnect tissue and various other structures, as well as covering it all with the extra flap of skin the two had been developing.

Three months prior to the operation, Ben and one of the other neurosurgeons traveled to Germany to implant a scalp expander in the children. This is a balloon-type device that is surgically placed under the skin, in this case between the two boys, and into which saline solution would be periodically injected. As the skin would be stretched, more would grow. Just prior to surgery, the children looked like they had another head! All that extra skin would be needed, however, because it would be used for both boys to cover the opening created by the separation.

Because there were essentially two patients, there were two teams of medical professionals, including neurosurgeons, anesthesiologists, cardiovascular surgeons, et cetera. Ben and Dr. Reginald Davis, one of the chief residents, worked on one twin, while Dr. Donlin Long, the chairman of the neurosurgery department, and the other chief resident, Dr. Sam Hassenbusch, worked on the other twin.

The surgery took twenty-two hours and there were some complications. One problem occurred right after the surgeons had completed the complex reconstruction in just under the one-hour limit. When the blood was recirculated through the babies, every place that could bleed did bleed. A baby's system typically has a fraction of the adult volume of six units of blood, and they lost so much that by the end of the operation they had gone through sixty units. When it looked like they were going to run out of blood after using fifty units, some of the seventy medical staff involved started offering their blood to save the twins. That wasn't practical, of course, but it was so generous-hearted. After hospital staff called all around the city of Baltimore, ten more units were finally found and the surgery could continue.

Due to the complexity and length of the surgery, some of the surgical teams could take breaks. For example, while the anesthesiologists were putting in lines to sedate the patients, the neurosurgeons didn't need to be in the room. During one of those periods, Ben and Reggie were in Ben's office to wait their turn to operate on the twins, chatting about this and that. Lo and behold, a while later, they suddenly woke up! They had fallen asleep in mid-conversation and happened to startle each other awake. The fact of the matter is, the grueling schedule these guys kept was enough to make anyone fall asleep. But as Ben always says, when it comes to a surgery that lasts ten, fifteen, twenty hours or more, it's like being in a jungle with a hungry tiger after you. Your adrenaline kicks in and you just keep going until things have calmed down, and then you collapse.

Little did Ben know that Dr. Long was impressed not only by his technical skill but by his humility in the situation. Years after the surgery, he wrote this account of the operation:

> Ben had personally been in charge of all the arrangements. He had invested an enormous amount of time in the organization, and yet as we were standing at the

table ready to start, he handed me the knife. We had two teams of surgeons and the composition is not commented about very often. Sam Hassenbusch and I were one team, Reggie Davis and Ben were the other.

As we got ready to start, Ben handed me the knife, a point that has been neglected in the history of all of the twins' publicity. I mentioned at one of the events, when Ben handed me the knife, he was testing me. Had I taken it and taken credit for the surgery, things would have been very different in Ben's career and at Johns Hopkins. My own actions would have been in keeping with the traditions of Neurosurgery and many predecessors. Now, knowing Ben, I had given some thought to this, because I expected him to do just what he did. He was being both deferential to a Chief, but he was also making sure that I had the opportunity to demonstrate what I thought about all such relationships. As I considered what I ought to do well before the surgery, I thought in some ways, "If I take the lead I will be protecting Ben from a bad outcome. What if they both die?" It will be headlines everywhere. I can take that heat at this stage in my career, but I am not sure that it is fair to Ben to let him run those risks. On the other hand, I thought, if we are successful it will make very little difference to my career, but will be an enormous advantage to Ben. And then I thought, Ben Carson does not need any protection. He has the talent and the skill and he has the emotional fortitude to stand up to any outcome. This is a remarkable opportunity for Ben, for me, for Neurosurgery and for Johns Hopkins. So, I handed the knife back as I am sure Ben expected. I have often used the "Carson Test" as an example when I have given talks around the world, indicating that the "Carson Test" is always "Will you do what is right, not what is expedient, and not what is personally advantageous?" If you will, you pass the "Carson Test." That's the message.

As Ben's wife, I deeply appreciated Dr. Long's generous, honest, and humble testimony. I wasn't with Ben day in and day out and didn't get to see him in surgery the way Dr. Long did, and his firsthand account meant the world to me, especially as it described such a historical landmark; this was the first successful separation of occipital craniopagus Siamese twins with both surviving in the world!

The Carsons in the Movies

Although the first two successful separations of Siamese twins took place about ten years apart (in 1986 and 1997), the stories were covered in several media outlets . . . so the word was out. The Farrelly brothers, Bobby and Peter, well known for their quirky comedic movies like *There's Something About Mary* and *Me, Myself & Irene*, were in the process of preparing for the production of a new movie based on the lifestyle of Siamese twins as well as a separation attempt. One of the producers, Bradley Thomas, who happened to be from the neighboring Maryland community of Reisterstown, had been working with the Farrelly brothers and suggested that they approach Ben to act in the movie as the surgeon who performs the operation. Of course Ben thought it was a hoax at first!

But Thomas is nothing if not persistent. Once he convinced Ben that it might be worth his while, we entered the world of Hollywood. The filming location was Fort Lauderdale, Florida, because the producers had located a hospital there with an unoccupied wing where filming could be done, eliminating a necessity to build sets. And they promised to film all of Ben's scenes in one day, as he couldn't take much time away from Hopkins.

We flew to Florida, left our bags at the hotel, and headed to the set, where we were told what to do. A couple of our kids wanted to wear T-shirts with logos of their choice, but they were told that would not be possible, because those kinds of endorsements are by contract only. So the Detroit and Tufts shirts were left in our hotel room and the boys were sent to wardrobe.

This totally unique experience was one you want to absorb every moment of and never forget. For one thing, it was interesting how they did meals there. Directors and actors had priority, as they had to be ready to get back on the set when parts were being filmed. Support people, like makeup artists, lighting, and sound and electrical engineers, were last. They had stunt doubles, but I thought it was interesting how they also had body doubles. These were individuals who had similar coloring, height, and body build to the principal actors. They would step in to ensure that lighting and stage placement were optimal before bringing the actual actors out to film a scene.

The boys and I were extras, actors without any speaking parts who are part of the backdrop of the scenes. Of course, the experience is one that will stay with us forever. It was interesting how the directors would always do at least five takes of a scene, if not ten, their reasoning being, "You might miss a small detail that is out of place"; how the lighting engineers were able to simulate daylight when it was close to midnight; and how friendly the stars were: Matt Damon even told our boys they could play video games in his trailer, and gave them autographed photos. It was an interesting experience to see Ben in a very different light as an actor. The skill set was completely different from his usual position of being in charge. As a chief in the medical arena, he had the responsibilities equivalent to a director in the movie business. But he had no problem changing to one of the players, for his natural humility kicked in and he was acting like a champ in no time! The boys and I were delighted to be a part of the movie-making process and noted as much detail as possible because it was a totally new and unique experience and would probably be our only chance to be involved in a movie like *Stuck on You.*

The Only Chance

As Ben's reputation grew, it was not uncommon for desperate parents to bring their ill children to Hopkins for a final chance at life. On one such occasion in 1986, the obstetrician of a woman who was pregnant with twins approached Ben to see if something could be done for her particular challenge. In this lady's case, the children were developing well except for one thing: one of the little ones had developed hydrocephalus, excess fluid on the brain. As the two children were growing, the head of the hydrocephalic twin was expanding too quickly, so much so that there was a chance that the children would be delivered early before they would be able to survive outside of the womb. The obstetrician knew that Ben had successfully operated on children with this same diagnosis who had already been born, installing a shunt to alleviate the life-threatening intracranial pressure the buildup of fluid could cause. His question was, would it be conceivable to perform this surgery on a child while he or she was still in the womb? Research on the matter revealed that intrauterine surgery had been successfully performed on sheep, but it had never been done on humans.

Over the years, Ben has developed an effective method of solving any dilemma. If you ask yourself four questions, you can usually come up with the best answer:

What's the best thing that will happen if I do this?

What's the worst thing that happens if I do this?

What's the best thing that will happen if I don't do this?

What's the worst thing that happens if I don't do this?

Once he went through those questions and considered the outcomes he realized that in this case the only chance at life for either of the children, but particularly the nonhydrocephalic child, was for him to shunt the one with the problem, to go ahead with the surgery. That was this child's *only* chance at life.

The mother was prepped, and the anesthesia was tricky. Too much could kill the babies, and too little would have the mother jumping during the procedure. Guided by ultrasound, the screen showed the progress of the shunt apparatus as it approached the growing bubble on the hydrocephalic twin. A special small, remotely controlled insertion tool installed the shunt successfully on the first try, and Ben later said that he could see the huge bubble begin to shrink instantly. It was a success! The size of the ill child's head would not continue to take up so much room that the children would have to be delivered before they were ready.

Postoperatively, the pregnancy continued to progress at the normal rate, and when the mother delivered, the healthy child was normal. But the bonus was that the hydrocephalic child was completely developed, too. Both twins had come out of the operation intact.

A little more than twenty years later, when I was attending a Youth for Christ dinner in Baltimore, a pretty young blond woman came up to me asking if I was Dr. Carson's wife. When I answered in the affirmative, she revealed that she was the shunted twin. I couldn't believe my eyes! This vibrant, gorgeous, intelligent young woman would not have been around if the obstetrician and Ben hadn't intervened. That was the first of many times that former patients have introduced themselves to me, thankful for my husband's work, helping me to appreciate him all the more and helping me to understand even better how the sacrifices were worth it.

Dedicated Coworkers and Colleagues

As Ben's department expanded, a couple more PAs were added and his administrative staff, headed by Audrey Jones, expanded to four. It never dawned on me that he was surrounded by women until a psychiatrist friend mentioned it, and reasoned that it must be hard for Ben to deal with their hormones. I guess you see what you're looking for. I knew for a fact from the times I would visit to bring him something he might have forgotten at home, or to deliver a birthday present or something like that, that these ladies were all dedicated and focused on getting their jobs done. With such a high patient load, and so many complex cases, there wasn't time for much of anything else. Occasionally I might hear them joke or razz each other a bit. But these were serious professionals, devoted to their jobs. To us, they were special, coworking friends.

The camaraderie and dedication of these coworkers was a fact of life, as I had witnessed this in brief interactions over the years.

But Dr. Long's reaction to the dedication of Ben's staff was one of extreme shock:

> I have never seen any faculty member at Hopkins whose behavior engendered such dedicated, unswerving support from all those who worked with him. All the secretaries, Carol James (Dr. Carson's senior physician assistant, or PA), and all the others that worked with Ben over the years were committed to his concepts and invested in helping his programs and him. I remember one day, Carol came to me as I was scrubbing in the room next to Pediatrics in Old Room 11. Ben was scrubbing next door and Carol came to say, "Dr. Long, we need some help. Ben is about to do his sixth case, including the emergencies that kept us up all night (in those days he averaged about ten operations per week). He is dead tired and we are not going to allow him to drive home. I will either take him home, or we are going to let him sleep in the office for a while before he makes any attempt to go home. Now I know he will do a superb job in the surgery, that is not my concern. My worry is that he is ruining his health with this schedule and we need to do something about it. We need more help in Pediatrics. Can I call you tonight if there are any issues with any of Ben's patients?" That was a unique event. I have never before heard any of the supporting personnel with whom my faculty worked express any personal concerns about the health and well-being of the boss. For a PA and secretaries to be arranging for the surgeon to get home

safely and to have an opportunity to sleep uninterrupt-
edly was really quite remarkable. It just demonstrates the
usual ways in which Ben interacted with his support
staff, in which the usual was in fact the most unusual,
almost unique. Ben's sincerity is obvious to those who
know him well, and they become as committed as he is.

For Dr. Long to say this when he served as the chief of neurosurgery for twenty-seven years is humbling, to say the least. But
when you consider Ben's above-and-beyond efforts for his staff,
Dr. Long's observations are less surprising. In 2000, Carol James
(Morton), Ben's senior physician assistant, who trained at Yale
University and is the godmother of our three sons, lost her mother,
with whom she was very close. She had succumbed to a swift,
unexpected, awful, and draining illness, and today was the day of
her memorial service. Carol could barely describe how tough it
had been to watch her beloved mother decline so rapidly. There
wasn't time to ponder good memories, and barely time to take care
of all the logistics connected with such a painful loss.

Carol, or CJ, as Ben called her, had been working in neurosurgery as Ben's right-hand person for eighteen years by that time. Ben
and I were traveling back to Baltimore the day of the funeral, and
Carol did not expect us to come, but we arrived close to the beginning. She recalled seeing us slip into the right aisle, and was warmed
by the fact that her boss had come almost directly from the airport
to honor her mother.

The service was comforting as they played her mother's favorite hymns, and presented a lovely eulogy. Carol had added another
dimension to the program. An announcement was made request-
ing anyone who was so moved to share their special memories of

the sweetheart of a woman whom she called "Mother." At first, no one moved. I think everyone was so touched by the service to that point, they were processing the fact that this dear friend, mentor, confidante, helper, and counselor was no longer with us.

Ben was the first to rise. He spoke of his memories of Mrs. James, and that one of the facets he valued most about her was that she had CJ, because CJ is and has been such an important part of his life. As he continued along in this vein, Carol was extremely moved. In a medical setting, she later told me, you work with people closely in life–and–death situations, and most times these high-stress interactions do not allow for niceties like "thank you" and "you're welcome." The patient's well-being comes first and fore-most, and there's a close bond that develops between team members responsible for that person's life. A special respect for one another is there, and each person has the other's back as far as the patient is concerned, but sometimes it's hard to fathom how this relationship translates to life outside the hospital.

For Ben to get up first, and speak of this heretofore undefined rela-tionship of respectful admiration and trust, was one thing that really touched Carol. But also because he got up first, and he was willing to start and break the ice by making it so personal that others in atten-dance were more comfortable sharing their special memories—this touched her even more. She was grateful that he took the time and initiative to share that appreciation for her dedication, wisdom in deal-ing with patients, and selfless actions throughout her career. It was to-tally unexpected, and came at a time when she really needed the words that usually couldn't be said for lack of time and concern for patients.

Audrey Jones, Ben's office manager, remembers Ben's kindness to patients and their families. Some time ago there was a beautiful boy about seven or eight years old from Nebraska with a malignant brain tumor. Ben had performed several surgeries on the child over the course of three years. This child was very mature, and knew he was very sick. It got to a point where it might be the last operation (and the most difficult one). Ben and the parents explained to the child that this surgery would be highly risky and that he might not make it. On the morning of the surgery as the orderlies rolled the boy into the OR, he said to his parents, "Just know that if I don't make it, I'll be watching over you from heaven." What a perspective from an eight-year-old! Although the surgery went well, the child never regained consciousness.

Audrey and one of the secretaries had developed a relationship with the family as they made arrangements for the child. They visited with the distraught mother when the child was in the pediatric intensive care unit (PICU), trying to ease her distress. Audrey was brought to tears as she witnessed the mother stroking the child's hand and desperately pleading, "Please wake up." This child had a younger brother he was very close to, and actually the entire family was very close.

It being Thanksgiving week, the family wanted to spend this last holiday together. They made a decision to mortgage their home and engaged a private medical evacuation helicopter with all the necessary equipment to transport the sick boy so he could be at home with family and not at a hospital when he died. Many hospital personnel thought this was a ridiculous decision and questioned the wisdom of mortgaging their home when the child was not going to be in this world much longer anyway, but Ben said, "They're doing what's right for them." Audrey could tell he felt for the parents while everyone else was saying, "Those folks are crazy for doing this."

It makes a difference when a doctor shows so much sympathy

and compassion. Over the years, Ben had a number of malignant brain tumor patients with quick death sentences, but he was able to extend either their lives or their quality of life by surgical intervention. Though he was always conservative with respect to surgery, comparing the benefits with the risks involved in each case, he firmly believed that the family's peace of mind and the patient's quality of life were of the utmost importance.

The child had been declared brain-dead, and Audrey noticed it was hard on Ben when he was asked when they would turn off the life support. He wanted to support the family's decision to have him at home, and they did for a couple of days. On Thanksgiving Day, at the end of the day, they turned off the life support.

Audrey remembers that Ben handled his grief and the grief of the parents with wisdom, tact, and kindness, as he always did. Being a physician is about more than technical ability, and even with a doctor who is technically gifted, a good bedside manner is very important. Ben was always gentle, even in the most horrific situations. He could make families feel better.

Do the Best You Can

Another of Ben's coworkers was Mary Kay Conover-Walker, a nurse practitioner who had worked with Ben while he was a resident, and continued with the department for more than twenty-five years. She noted that when a crisis arose, Ben would talk very quietly and deliberately with excellent eye contact and was warm in his expression. She remembered situations where "everything can be coming down around us," and Ben would say something like,

"Well, Mary Kay, everything will be fine. We have to concentrate on the problems and fix them." She shared a particularly telling story about a patient whom she had grown very close to.

> I recall speaking to Ben in the Meyer 7 hallway one day after I had come from a patient's room. The patient was an older teen who had been a longtime patient in neurosurgery. She and I had become very close. During this admission, it was clear that she was rapidly declining due to her enlarging, inoperable posterior fossa tumor. I was near tears. I told Ben about her decline and was very upset. He gently said to me, "Mary Kay, she is dying." At the time I was taken aback, I did not want an answer like that. But as I looked at Ben with tears in my eyes, he told me, "Your goal is to prevent infection and make her remaining life as comfortable as possible. I want you to be sure you are meticulous in your hand washing and wound care. Sometimes you have to realign your goals based on the prognosis. Your goals have to be realistic. She is not going to be cured. But you can make a difference in her life." It was hard to hear, but that conversation changed my nursing practice for the rest of my life. I am grateful for that discussion. I will never forget it.

This manner of approaching a less than optimal medical situation brings to mind our Australian neighbor Dr. Phil Clingan, an oncologist who could be positive when facing the worst type of cancer in any of his patients. It's difficult for any of us to face dire situations. By always doing your best, making life as good for the patient as you possibly can, you are addressing their needs. Life is not always perfect and many times things do not go the way you want them to, but as long as you do the best you can do for that patient, you have done your job with compassion. And in the event that a new medical cure is discovered prior to their demise, that patient will benefit.

Dr. Vining's Memories

In the late 1980s Johns Hopkins fostered the concept of "child life," the philosophy of patient-centered care, where the whole patient was cared for, and many steps were taken to make the medical experience less painful for the child. People from that department would work alongside the physicians to preserve as much quality of life for the children as possible. Dr. Freeman (then neurology chief) led by example, getting on the floor, playing with the children, and in the process giving them a neurologic exam without their knowing it.

Ben's philosophy meshed well with the concept and he was an enthusiastic holistic health proponent, as Dr. Patti Vining remembers. Dr. Vining is the recently retired head of Johns Hopkins' Pediatric Epilepsy Center. She graduated from Johns Hopkins Medical School in 1972 and was possibly the first female neurologist at Hopkins Medical Institutions. She became the director of pediatric neurology in 2011 and served in that position for several years before retiring.

Dr. Vining shared a story of a little girl not yet a year old who had been born with a brain where one side was not normally developed. The prescribed surgery that was done was complex and intricate, but successful, and after ensuring that she was stable, the operating team continued with their other work and at the end of the day left for their respective homes. Dr. Vining was still at the hospital when her intuition sent her back to that child's room for one last check before she left, to make sure all was copacetic. Something was wrong. She called Ben, but by the time he got back to the hospital, the baby had not survived. It was really tough on the family, and it wasn't easy for the doctors either. But Dr. Vining said she doesn't recall any families Ben was dealing with ever being angry at him. She thought it had to do with Ben's "calm, soothing nature."

Whenever things went wrong, Ben would immediately start asking, "Why? Why did it go wrong? Where can we find a reason why and how can we improve? How can we fix it for the future?" That spirit was one that he expected of each one on the team. He hated to see things go bad and wanted to make sure mistakes were never repeated. In that particular case, after careful study of the situation, it was determined that a dedicated pediatric anesthesia person should be utilized the entire time in pediatric cases. They had learned from the tragedy.

Although Dr. Vining and Ben are not in agreement politically, she generously described him this way, "He disarmed people with his presence . . . his slight build kept him from being too imposing a figure, his demeanor was always calm, and his eyes would connect with people, silently reassuring, 'I see you, I hear you,' putting them at ease."

Trainees

Dr. Violette Renard Recinos is head of pediatric neurosurgical oncology at the world-renowned Cleveland Clinic in Ohio. This coveted position was hard earned. She did her residency training at Johns Hopkins Medical Center under Ben and recalled that she first met Ben in the summer between her sophomore and junior years as an undergrad neuroscience major at Johns Hopkins University in 1996.

A starry-eyed undergraduate, drawing closer to achieving her dream of becoming a doctor, she hoped to take advantage of the fact that her undergraduate school was connected to one of the most well-known bastions of excellence in medicine, Johns Hopkins Medical Center. She really wanted to be a doctor, particularly a neurosurgeon. And because her undergraduate school was connected with one of the leading hospitals in the country for neurosurgery, she dreamed of shadowing and/or working with one of the professors in that department. Going through the regular process of applications, interviews, and referrals, she was ecstatic when she landed a research internship with Dr. Richard North, a neurosurgeon.

When her friends found out she would be working in the neurosurgery department, they were wide-eyed with excitement for her: "Maybe you'll have a chance to see Dr. Carson!" To which Violette replied, "Who is he? Aren't they all great?" Her friends' eyes got even bigger as they responded, "You don't know Dr. Carson? Why, he's the one you hear about on the news and in all the newspapers who does all this pioneering surgery, like taking out half a person's brain for seizures, and implanting shunts to relieve the pressure on the brain from hydrocephalus!" A friend actually gave her a copy of Ben's book *Gifted Hands*, which she completed in short order.

During the summer as she was working in Dr. North's laboratory, she would sometimes pass by the ORs and notice the schedule posted near the door listing the surgeons who would be operating that day. When she saw Ben's name, she wondered out loud, "I wonder if I can ever actually see an operation." Dr. David Antezana, a resident passing by, said, "Well, sure. Yeah. Why don't you come in?" She said she was so nervous to be able to see this Dr. Carson she had only read about. Standing by the wall, she waited and waited for him to come to the OR while the patient was being prepped. She was expecting him to act like some celebrity, but in her words, "He was acting all normal . . . like he is . . . quiet, polite, very friendly, asking people how they were doing." He could have totally ignored her and she would have been happy just to watch. He actually took time to acknowledge the young visitors in the room (there were a couple of other student observers who had been allowed in as well). When he asked their names, she noticed that he remembered the correct pronunciation, because a little later he called her to come a bit closer to see what they were doing.

She added, "No one ever pronounces my name correctly! Ever!" And he explained patiently the child's condition. He even engaged her in conversation and asked her directly, "Violette, so you're a neuroscience major. Do you know what this is? Or what this might be? So what do you want to do when you grow up?"

The line of questioning that made the most distinct impression on her came after she told him she wanted to be a neurosurgeon. "Why do you want to be a neurosurgeon? Do you know how much work is involved? Let me ask you, do you want to have a family? Do you want to have children?" Her answers in the affirmative yielded his reply: "Well, maybe you don't want to be a neurosurgeon."

Carol James was there and chimed in, "But you have a family, Dr. C." And he said, "Well, I have a wife. And Violette, you will need to have a husband who will be willing to help care for the family. This is not to say that you can't be a neurosurgeon and have a family, but it's going to take a lot of work. Some that do it have grandparents nearby to help raise the children. What would be good for you is to marry an engineer, or someone like that with a predictable schedule and similar education." She really resonated with those words. Others' responses to her declaration of the desire to become a neurosurgeon were along the lines of "You go, girl!"

Ben was the first to give her a more realistic view of what to expect. He wasn't saying that she couldn't do it, but that it would require much more work than most would expect—it's not easy. And the fact is, nobody can replace Mommy. Violette felt it was important for her to hear this from him. Even now, when she gets home her little ones "fight" over who Mommy will put to bed; she has a rotating schedule to keep everyone happy.

Ben invited the students to come back anytime, and treated them well, making them feel important. Years later, when she was a resident fellow in the neurosurgery department, Violette's niece came to Baltimore to shadow Ben, and Violette recalls that he treated her niece the same as he had the other students and herself several years ago.

She said this was her most impactful encounter with Ben.

Pablo Recinos is a neurosurgeon at the Cleveland Clinic who just so happened to marry Violette Renard, the neurosurgeon you just read about. Both trained at Johns Hopkins, and Ben mentored both of them. Pablo said he had many fond memories of Ben, but a couple in particular came to the forefront of his mind. The first time he heard Ben speak, he didn't know what he was expecting, but with Ben's soft voice and humble attitude he didn't expect the message to be so forceful. It was a message of confidence. Ben said, "In order to seek out what you want, you have to be a leader, first for yourself. If you can't lead yourself, you can't lead others. And learn how to take the initiative. Don't just stand by while things happen. Good things don't happen just because you're a good person." A casual listener might have thought Ben was overconfident, but his aim was to motivate residents to achieve much more than they might otherwise. He would always try to bring out the confidence in the residents so they could accomplish great things.

In an operation where Pablo was assisting Ben, the patient had trigeminal neuralgia, an extremely painful condition of the face. One of the remedies is an operation called a microvascular decompression. The pain emanates from an artery pressing against the trigeminal nerve. The procedure starts with opening the dura (brain covering), then delicately navigating the space between the cerebellum and petrous bone inside, following that corridor down to the trigeminal nerve and inserting a Teflon pledget (a small wad) to act as a cushion between the artery and the nerve. This is all under a highly magnified operating microscope. It can take three or more hours to complete this surgery, depending on how much scarlike arachnoid tissue is in the pathway to the nerve. Pablo said, "This area is full of potential land mines . . . there are other important nerves in that area . . . a slip of the scalpel could cause a stroke . . . it's a very delicate area where all kinds of neurological problems could erupt with a slight move in the wrong direction." This operation is one that Pablo had seen Ben perform many times, and as a second-year resident he had assisted Ben with this operation on several occasions.

"As a teacher Ben had tremendous patience, allowing the residents to do surgical procedures as he oversaw the operations." But Pablo also noted with admiration that Ben had a special sixth sense, because without anyone saying anything, he would somehow know when to take the scalpel in hand himself. If a resident was going a bit slowly, Ben's humor would kick in as he would say something like, "It's okay if you remove cell layer by cell layer to get to the bone."

This particular time prior to surgery, Ben had hurt his thumb, and Pablo could see Ben struggling due to his pain. He would position himself in different ways to make it work, but Pablo could tell the pain was difficult for him to deal with and do the surgery well. Ben's sixth sense kicked in again as he felt that perhaps Pablo was ready to take over, so he asked him, "Do you feel equipped to sit in this chair now?"

Pablo realized that at this point Ben could have called an upper-level resident or faculty member to come and take over, but he didn't. He looked Pablo in the eye and made the offer. It was the first time Pablo took over for Dr. C, and the one time he dictated every step (even though Pablo had seen it before). Still, the responsibility was Ben's. At the end, Ben complimented Pablo: "What you've done today is above the level of training where you are and you did a very nice job. I have confidence in you, Pablo." Ben had believed that there wouldn't be any risk, because Pablo did not do things recklessly, taking great care and time. Ben also knew Pablo would stop and ask questions if he had any concerns. "These lessons in the perception and sensitivity of the teacher for the resident's level of skill and confidence are coming to my mind these days as I teach the next generation of neurosurgeons," Pablo shared.

Stories like these explain the affection Dr. Long observed in Ben's staff toward him. Ben treats everyone well, and his kindness and wisdom have earned that kind of devotion.

Surgical "Talent Scout"

Another situation involving complex surgery was described by Dr. Henry Brem, a colleague who joined the neurosurgical service at the same time as Ben did and who became the director of the department of neurosurgery in 2000. He shared, "Ben is one who always likes to improve on things. His focus is always about how he can make something better or quicker or more efficient." In this case another set of craniopagus twins needed to be separated. Unlike the first set, this set of type 1 conjoined Siamese twins were connected at the top of the head.

In thinking about the best way to proceed this time, it came to Ben that at Hopkins, here was the best neurosurgery department in the United States (according to *U.S. News & World Report*). Why not take advantage of that fact? Instead of doing the whole operation himself with just a few others, why not utilize the talents of each neurosurgeon in the department to the best advantage?

"Ben actually brought everyone together to discuss the procedures in detail and the plan for everyone to get involved. He had several planning meetings, in effect acting like a war strategist," Dr. Brem said. "We all worked under Ben's direction. Although any one of the neurosurgeons could have done the entire surgery by themselves, each one has their own area of expertise within the field of neurosurgery. Some were best at neurovascular cases, some with craniofacial reconstruction, some with tumors and tissue separation, others were great at skull-base surgery, et cetera. Ben's hope and plan was to utilize those special skills of each neurosurgeon in the most effective way. And after explaining the plan and some discussion, every single one of the authoritarian neurosurgeons agreed to participate in the manner in which the plan was laid out. They were each willing to subjugate their usual way of working independently, being in command themselves, of running their own operating room with everyone else in that room assisting them, to working together as a team toward the common goal of separating this set of Siamese twins. Each one of the team members felt it was all about working together for the common good." Dr. Brem stated, "This is an outstanding example of leadership. Nothing before or since has ever drawn the whole department together!"

Dr. Brem's admiration of how Ben was able to inspire his colleagues to lay aside their egos and work together clearly showed in his voice.

"Ben came up with the idea of surgical shifts, with designated neurosurgical goals, and having each group of neurosurgeons operate at the point in the process where their expertise would be most applicable. This was designed to utilize the specific specialized talents of each one. And no matter how good each surgeon still felt after his/her portion of the operation, they would step aside as agreed, to allow the next group to accomplish the successive neurological goal. Keep in mind this is totally against their nature. Typically, a neurosurgeon would keep going, no matter how tired he was. It was drummed into them during their extensive training that it's much more important to continue and make sure the patient's problems are solved or at least stabilized before stopping to take a break and leaving the room. After decades of practicing this philosophical approach to surgery, now they were being asked to do shift work! Totally unheard of! There was never a surgical experience like this! The team effort was bigger than any one of the neurosurgical stars that each one of these surgical practitioners could honestly claim to be!"

Dr. Brem concluded that this was "*one of the most memorable events in Hopkins' history.*" There were eighteen neurological surgeons involved.

I was later told that due to this strategy, the operation was ten hours ahead of schedule! Being able to recognize others' strengths and talents as well as having the willingness to allow them to utilize them are special talents of a true leader.

Special Recognition?

It wasn't always just friendly people who testified to Ben's qualities. As he became increasingly famous, I was intrigued to see some unusual responses to him. One particular account I didn't see, but he told me about. On his way home from the hospital one evening when he was on staff, it was early, the sun hadn't set yet, and Ben was delighted to be going home in time for dinner with everyone. He was driving his latest "baby," a sleek new 1991 royal blue Jaguar Sovereign. He stopped by a gas station close to the hospital, parked the car, and went into the station to prepay for the gas. As he walked from the station to pump gas in the car, he noticed two young men in it beginning to drive it away. Quickly, he ran to the car. They hadn't picked up speed yet. Before Ben could say anything, the guys paused and asked, "Say, are you that doctor? That one from Johns Hopkins?" After shifting the gears to park the would-be car thieves got out of the car and shook his hand, saying, "It's so nice to meet you! It's an honor! We're so glad to be able to shake your hand!" And with that they gave the car back.

Family Friendships

Not only did I learn a lot about Ben from his colleagues and from those who recognized him, but I learned a lot about him from our family friends, one of whom he made very early in his career. Sometimes as the head of pediatric neurosurgery at one of the top medical centers in the world, he was called upon to be an expert witness in malpractice cases involving neurosurgical procedures. It was helpful extra income because we were still paying off college loans. And Ben found that he thoroughly enjoyed the experience. When a prosecuting lawyer would attempt to lead him to a conclusion that he wanted, Ben could see where he was going and avoid the trap the lawyer was trying to spring. Typically the lawyer would try it several different ways to get Ben to say exactly what he wanted, but Ben wasn't buying it. All those years of studying psychology were kicking in, and Ben's perceptions and sensitivity to what was going on were on high alert.

One memorable example of this was when a lawyer actually came to Ben's office to get a deposition. Ben could tell from the manner in which the questions were asked that this guy had more than a little knowledge of neurosurgery. It turns out that this lawyer, Dr. Harvey Wachsman, had been a neurosurgeon, but switched his career to law and became a malpractice attorney. He had even been elected president of the American Board of Professional Liability Attorneys, a position he held for eighteen years!

Continuing the verbal dance, Harvey would lead the conversation one way, and Ben would parry and switch the conversation to another direction and vice versa. They had such a good time that once they had completed the deposition, Harvey declared that would be the last time they would be on opposite sides. He invited our family to join his for Christmas that year on Long Island, New York, and that was the first of many lovely holidays shared. His and his lawyer-wife Kathryn's children were of similar ages to our three sons, and we all got along very well. There were excellent conversations over dinner, and fun chasing the dogs around the house. Their poodle Popcorn was a favorite for all.

We'd often go to the opera at the Met and take in the dramatic musicals. Sometimes the kids would go too, especially if the program was a child-themed matinee. They all went to see *The Lion King*. And the box that Harvey maintained there is in the center of the balcony with a fabulous view of the entire stage. It had been the seat of various prestigious patrons, so it had historical significance.

Our children got along well together. Our families' two eldest sons, Murray and David, were inseparable. And our youngest, Rhoeyce, and their youngest son, Derek, were especially great buddies. One time as we were preparing to depart, Rhoeyce hid so we didn't have to leave. He didn't want the fun times to end! We all spent about half an hour looking for him before he got the lecture!

One particular Christmas, their oldest daughter, Dara, who had completed her undergraduate degree at the University of Michigan in three years, had just finished her course at Le Cordon Bleu in Paris. Her mother enjoyed cooking, as did her grandparents, and she and her two sisters had developed quite a bit of expertise as well. When Dara had the opportunity to expand her horizons in that world, and at such a prestigious and highly selective school, she took advantage of it. So she was in charge of the kitchen that Christmas.

On the morning after we got there, she had planned on preparing special pancakes with the Cordon Bleu flair. As she began assembling ingredients, however, she could not locate the recipe. Kathryn, the girls, and I looked everywhere we thought it could be, but realized quickly that if breakfast was going to be anywhere near on time, we needed to implement Plan B . . . and soon. Fortunately, my cousin Val Battle had shared a recipe for pancakes that became a family favorite. Although the pancakes were whole wheat, the texture was light and fluffy and they had a tinge of cinnamon flavor to make them even more tasty. This recipe was such a favorite that I was able to write it down from memory and Dara did not mind using it. No one told Harvey or the other guests. When he exclaimed over the Cordon Bleu pancakes and asked, "Have you ever tasted any with such great flavor?" we didn't disabuse him of his notion. It was our little secret. Ben commented later, "I wonder what Harvey would have done if he had found out they weren't from the Cordon Bleu?"

We've kept up through the years, even though we haven't been able to do Christmases together because the children have grown up and developed their own schedules. But their sons were in our sons' weddings in 2011. Their friendship has enriched our lives and made me appreciate Ben even more.

Ben on Board

As a Yalie I was more than happy to vote for Ben when he was in the running for a place on the university's board of directors. When the results came in, he had been elected a trustee of the Yale Corporation, and this occurred the same year he began service as a board member of the Kellogg Company in 1997, from which he resigned in 2015. He also served on the Costco board for sixteen years and was a member of the board of Regent University for a number of years as well. He thoroughly enjoyed the challenges, working on various problems with other intellectuals, putting their heads together, looking at issues from different perspectives, and coming up with optimal solutions. He was in his element! And with some boards, they would have family days and the kids and I would enjoy meeting and interacting with the other families involved.

One time when Ben was away at a Yale board meeting, we came up with a surprise for him upon his return. The boys and I had recently formed our family string quartet, the Carson 4. Ben was due to return home from one of those meetings one Sunday afternoon and we thought it would be nice to welcome him home with a mini concert. So I called the airport authority, got permission to play, and was directed verbally to the location near his arrival gate where we should set up and at what time. We were all in place with stands, chairs, music books, with instruments tuned and at the ready near the gate where Ben was to disembark. (This was in the days before the TSA.) As the door to the jetway opened we began playing, and what a look on Ben's face. He was totally surprised. One of the other board members said she was jealous—she had never had a concert to welcome her home! And of course Ben said he'd share his.

One unexpected result of Ben's joining the boards was a change in his diet. As I mentioned earlier, both Ben and I had become vegetarians in college and had continued in that diet since then. That changed after Ben joined the boards. It bothered him that the caterers had to bend over backward to come up with vegetarian meals for him. He felt bad that they would have to go to a lot of trouble to come up with something, and he'd prefer not to cause anyone extra trouble. So he started including fish and chicken in his diet.

Carson Christmases

Christmastime was especially festive when we would host the entire neurosurgery department and their families at our house. It was one of the two times during the year when not only the house staff, but spouses, children, and sometimes parents would all congregate and relax together. Nurses, techs, physician assistants, and their families were invited as well, rounding out the total in attendance to between seventy and one hundred. It was a great opportunity for the families of the department to get to know one another and for me to get to know the people who spent time with Ben at the hospital.

We were games people, so at the center of each table would be the requisite holiday centerpiece as well as a group game, like Guesstures, Taboo, or Mad Gab, mostly to break the ice for those who hadn't gotten to know one another yet. And it was open seating, so often people who hadn't yet become acquainted would be at the same table.

The event would be held on a Saturday evening in our open lower level, with crimson poinsettia garlands around the white pillars, Christmasy tablecloths, evergreen garlands on the billiard table light, et cetera. And the big-screen TV would be in full view from any section of the area with the sound turned down for the guys (and gals) who didn't want to miss any of any pertinent football games that were going on. The buffet was set up on the serving area between the kitchen and the "great room" so that everyone could serve themselves and get settled among the round cheerily decorated tables.

The crowning event for the party was the Olde Fashioned

Yankee Gift Exchange. Others may know this by another name, but the way it worked, each adult guest would bring a wrapped gift of a predetermined value marked according to gender, and it would be placed on one of the red-tablecloth-covered tables under the big-screen TV. Each adult guest would also draw a number from a basket that one of our boys would be carting around. Ben would explain the rules of the game and start by calling out the highest number. Then the guest with that number could select any gift he or she wanted from the entire collection, unwrap it, and hold it up for all to see. He or she would then sit down and wait to see if it remained in his/her possession. This was because each subsequent guest would select a gift from the pile, unwrap it, and show it off, but if a previously selected gift caught their eye, they could exchange their gift for any previously opened one, no questions asked. Some gifts would hop around quite a bit before the game was over. Ben became known for his humorous commentary about how long it took for someone to open a gift, or for warning a guest who had a gift that seemed to be popular that they might not be holding on to it for much longer.

We also provided gifts for the children, who would draw from another set of numbers. I learned quickly that the children needed their own separate time, to avoid tears and long waits in between the adults' turns. When we first started this practice, I would try to wrap the gifts, basically a time-consuming and unproductive task, because most times I would not get the total number of children, ages, and genders until the evening prior to the event (these medical people had a few other things on their minds besides whether their children could attend a party or not), which left me with a huge shopping and wrapping chore at the last minute. With twenty to thirty children's gifts, it was virtually impossible to get them all wrapped in time, before the guests arrived.

So I created a Christmas-tree-shaped display of graduated tables covered by a green blanket, festooned with blue and silver garland. Their gifts were displayed unwrapped according to the children's heights. Babies' and toddlers' gifts were on the lowest and broadest shelf of the "tree," and were usually stuffed toys or blankets, that sort of thing. The teen gifts (up through age fourteen) were on the top, smaller tiers of the tree. Children were allowed to examine the gifts as long as their parents would let them, but there were no exchanges. Again, early on we discovered another fact of life: little ones don't appreciate having to let their treasures go. So once they had their toy, they could play with it all they wanted and take it home with them. We would have the children's "exchange" first, so the little ones would be content and patient while the longer, more involved adult exchange took place.

With the schedule being what it was, we usually hosted the Scholars Fund board meeting and party the following morning, so it was clean up and re–set up that night after everyone had gone home. We were always tired after these weekends, but they were also very much worth the effort. It was a way of celebrating the combined achievements of the year for the neurological staff as well as the volunteer efforts and successes of our charity's board. And their families got to celebrate this with them. Our children helped with the events and enjoyed having more kids around to play with! And I got to hear from those who saw Ben more than I did. It was heartwarming to see so many dedicated hard workers enjoying themselves and also fun to see them let their hair down! It was a special Christmas present for me.

Reunion

Another situation where I got to learn about Ben from people who knew him in a different way was a few years back when Ben and I had the opportunity to attend his twenty-fifth high school reunion in Detroit. Prior to this it had been difficult to attend any reunions of any kind; the schedule just didn't allow it. If he was curious as to what this reunion would be like, he wasn't much more curious than I was. I had seen photos he had collected at the graduation of classmates, and he had shared interesting anecdotes about the shenanigans he and his classmates were involved in. I couldn't wait.

Everyone was decked out in their evening wear—it was almost like going back to a prom. As members of the class of 1969 recognized one another, shouts of joy in the recognition, disbelief at how they hadn't (or in actuality had) changed, and fond memories returning to life echoed around the room, while spouses like me kind of sat back watching their antics in amazement. With chest bumps between football teammates and pogo stick–like jumping up and down by former cheerleaders, it was like these folks were back in high school.

As the evening continued and the program started, the camaraderie of the class grew. The inevitable walks down memory lane that each speaker brought to the audience unearthed memories, some of which might have been better off remaining in the past. Many were bittersweet, but most were fun, positive, and smile-eliciting.

Afterward we had a chance to catch up with Ben's main rival during high school, Tim McDaniel, who had become an attorney. From what they were saying, he and Ben were always competing for the highest mark on every exam, quiz, test, paper, you name it. It was a healthy competition, though, and probably made it more fun for them both as they went through the rigors of high school.

The most intriguing element was the memory of the students who used to tease Ben mercilessly about being a nerd, for now they were all saying, "Don't you remember how we used to encourage you?" and "We tell our kids all about you." Funny how memories can change over the years. But the message is the same: "Do your best, and you will be blessed."

And that has been the guiding principle of Ben's life. He has blessed others, in his family, at work, and abroad, and has truly been blessed in return. His bosses, subordinates, friends, and former "enemies" alike praise his character, confirming that the man I see at home is the same man everywhere he goes.

Chapter 11

New Perspectives

In 2002, Ben noticed that the clock was becoming more important to him while he was in the OR. He was feeling the need to leave to use the restroom, and that was unusual for him. So he made an appointment to see his friend the chief of urology, Dr. Pat Walsh. In reassuring tones, Dr. Walsh said it was probably nothing to worry about. After the testing, Ben's PSA was a little high, so Dr. Walsh suggested that they take some biopsies. When Ben tells this story, at this point he stops and says, "If anyone ever tells you that a biopsy doesn't hurt . . . it doesn't hurt *them*. They leave out that portion of the sentence. After about six biopsies, I'm thinking cancer isn't that bad, just stop with the biopsies."

Despite his reservations, Ben had all the biopsies his urologist requested. The samples were sent to the lab for evaluation, and Ben instructed them to let him know the results as soon as the information was available. He was in the OR working on someone's brain when the call came through. One of the nurses put the phone up to his ear and he was told that not only was it a tumor, but it was a high-grade aggressive carcinoma.

A follow-up MRI was done, but they really didn't expect to find anything else. Ben received the scan results as he left to go to his office. Usually the person delivering the scans will say something positive like "We didn't find anything," but the delivery person was dead silent as he handed them to Ben. When he put the scans on the view box, Ben's heart sank as he saw multiple lesions running up and down his spine. The cancer appeared to have metastasized.

First he checked the name on the scan to make sure it was his. And he reluctantly accepted the fact that it was. Then he thought, "Well, I've had a good life, and the children are mostly grown." Shortly afterward, Carol James, his senior physician assistant, came into the room, certain that the problem was not severe, saying, "Let me see, let me see." And she abruptly stopped before the board as her face fell when she recognized the lesions as well.

Funny how quickly news travels. The next day in the newspaper it said that Ben had a glioblastoma, a malignant tumor on the brain—that's the other end. Other news outlets said he had lung cancer, kidney cancer, bone cancer . . . as he says in his speeches, "You name it, I had it." One person called the office and said, "I heard Dr. Carson was dead . . . I want to talk to him!"

However, there was a wonderful outpouring of prayer and many calls and letters came in support, from janitors and ancillary medical personnel all the way up to President and Mrs. Bush. People also sent all kinds of healing potions, vitamins, grasses, et cetera, to help. At least five bags of mail filled with get-well cards and well wishes arrived at the office.

With all the prayer, and by watching his diet and vitamins closely,

Ben started feeling much better. He was even thinking about not going through with the prescribed surgery. From his perception of his general health, it really felt like the prayers were being answered to the point where the cancer was receding. But then he thought it probably would not set a good example for him to elect not to go through with the surgery, because others with similar prognoses might not take their conditions seriously enough to do what is really necessary to overcome the disease. So he decided to go ahead.

He was scheduled for surgery early in the day. Boy, was it weird to see him as a patient, in a patient's gown and not in his professor's coat with his name on the pocket. I think he felt somewhat weird, too. Imagine being in your workplace, where you usually have control, and then having to turn over everything to someone else. I think he was starting to understand more fully how patients feel—the indignity of those gowns alone makes quite an impression on the psyche.

I had to wait in a waiting room like everyone else. Ben's best friend had come to be there for him and waited with me. When the surgeon came to tell us the outcome a few hours later, the anticipation was palpable. But the news was good. All went well. He even informed us of the magnitude of the tumor. It had come to within a millimeter of breaking through the prostate; it had been totally encapsulated within the organ. So the radical nerve-sparing prostatectomy developed by Dr. Pat Walsh and performed by him had done the job!

Ben was groggy but happy when we finally got to see him. And he was so happy to be able to leave the hospital and get back to his own bed.

Ben recovered, went right back to work, and remained busy with surgeries but also began speaking more, and we started thinking about retirement. This is something he had been threatening to do for several years, but perhaps this time it would actually happen. Our sons all married in 2011, and we were getting close to the next stage of life. Our lifestyle changed as we noticed America changing right before our eyes and Ben began thinking about how to wake up America. Our country was becoming something totally different from what the founding fathers had envisioned. We were losing our hard-fought-for freedoms. So we began traveling to three or four states a week, attempting to rouse our fellow citizens.

As Ben neared retirement age, we began to wonder what really would be next. We were looking forward to retirement, but we also knew that we didn't want to abandon lives of service. We'd become increasingly aware that we were in a position to help others, and Ben had been in a few situations that developed an impression in his mind that maybe his particular purpose in life was to help America wake up.

Gifted Hands

"Doctor, you have to do something!" This was the impassioned plea of the parents of a four-year-old boy who could no longer walk. From the scans it looked like he had a tumor on his brain stem. The family had come all the way from Georgia after having traveled the country in search of a neurosurgeon who could help them. Ben reviewed the scans and confirmed the diagnosis: malignant tumor of the brain stem. "There's nothing I or anyone else can do about this," he said. "It's an inoperable tumor in the worst place possible."

"But Doctor," the mother responded, "we came all this way to find a Christian neurosurgeon who could help us. We prayed about this. The Lord is going to heal our son, and he's going to use you to do it!"

Ben paused and finally spoke. "Well, perhaps we can try an MRI. This is a new diagnostic test that might reveal something other than what this appears to be."

After the parents agreed, the young man was taken to neuroradiology for the MRI, prepped, and the test was done. The results? The same as before: a malignant tumor on the brain stem. The parents still pressured Ben, saying, "But, Doctor, the Lord is going to heal our son!" Their persistence wasn't lost on Ben, and after musing a bit, he suggested, "Maybe if we take a biopsy it will show something that we're missing." The parents eagerly agreed, hoping for any chance for their cherished only son. The sample was extracted and sent off to be checked. While the lab was completing the tests to determine the composition of the tumor, Ben decided he might as well debride it, take as much out as possible to prolong the little guy's life.

When the results of this latest test came back, it was like a broken record: "high-grade carcinoma of the brain stem." After closing the opening, the medical team took the boy back to the PICU. Ben was sad to have to deliver the bad news, especially when the parents were so hopeful. He started with the usual things a doctor says to reassure the parents: "Maybe your son has served his purpose in life, perhaps he has done all God wanted him to do, we'll all understand it better by and by. . . ." But they still came back with the same refrain: "Thank you, Doctor, but the Lord is going to heal our son." And Ben could only reply, "Your faith is admirable!"

Fully expecting the child to deteriorate from the terrible invasion of his cranium, Ben was surprised when in a few days, the boy started to improve! His eyes became conjugate—that is, they looked in the same direction—he was starting to be able to handle his secretions (no more foaming at the mouth), and his motor skills were clearly returning. Ben was thrilled and suggested another MRI to see what was going on.

The MRI showed that the tumor was still there, but the brain stem appeared to be smashed to one side as opposed to being invaded by the tumor. Ben's optimism rose as he noted the possibility that the tumor was still outside of the brain stem, not inside. He proposed going back in to see, and the parents agreed.

It wasn't too tough getting down to that brain stem, all the way to the base of the skull, as it was a procedure Ben had done many times. But as he got closer to the destination, there were a lot of abnormal blood vessels in the area to navigate. After a tedious journey through them, there it was: a glistening white brain stem, smashed to one side but still intact. And the constitution of the tumor had changed as well. It was no longer soft, with the consistency of cheese grits, but was much firmer. It had changed so significantly that Ben was able to peel it off the delicate brain stem layer by layer until they reached it. The brain stem started to regain its original shape almost immediately after the tumor was removed. The somber mood of the OR quickly changed to one of joyous expectation! The team repaired the tissue, vessels, and other important structures and closed the wound, exhilaration flooding those who had a part in helping to restore this young man's journey on his way back to good health.

The boy continued to improve, and one of the neurooncologists actually came up to Ben shortly afterward and said, "Ben, I've always been an atheist up until now. But after watching this whole thing unfold, I am now a believer."

And of course the parents were ecstatic! Their prayers had been answered in a big way. They were getting their son back. This little boy who had shown so much promise was going to continue down a special path that had been laid out especially for him. Reciting Bible verses from age two, and preaching by age four, this little fellow's life was absolutely *not* over with, as so many had declared.

The other health care professionals' responses up to this point were reflective of their appreciation of the situation. But Ben's realization was a particularly significant one for him. He had thought in the back of his mind that he was really "hot stuff." He had been trained at Yale University and at one of the best medical schools in the country, the University of Michigan. To then be admitted into a surgical residency program where only 2 were chosen out of 125 applicants, and *then* to become the chief of pediatric neurosurgery at a major teaching medical institution like Johns Hopkins at the tender age of thirty-three would go to a guy's head for sure. He knew he was really something else! However, this little boy and his problem brought Ben to his knees, mentally. Ben knew he had nothing to do with the consistency of that tumor changing. He knew that the area of the brain stem is not something you mess with. There are so many things that could go wrong. If he had breathed too deeply during the surgery, the outcome for this little boy could have been death. A sneeze might have given the child a stroke or worse. Ben *knew* for certain then Who the Surgeon really was. "From this point on," Ben prayed, "I'll let You be the Surgeon, God . . . and I'll be the hands." This revelation was where the title for Ben's autobiography, *Gifted Hands,* came from.

Spared for a Purpose

The miracle of the Georgia child's brain stem tumor changing was yet another confirmation that Ben had been spared for a purpose. Having performed around fifteen thousand surgeries in his career, it was clear that God had him in mind to serve as a healer. So many unexplained miracles occurred in many of those surgical procedures. And Ben's life had been miraculously spared a few times, too, even before his victory over cancer.

One time, years earlier, Ben was to speak in the Bahamas in the city of Freeport and the family was with him as was the custom for us. After the speech was over, Ben was approached by some of the leaders from Nassau, who off the cuff invited him to speak there. They said, "You can't come all this way and not come speak to us too!" It just so happened that one of the kids wasn't feeling well, so the three boys, Ben's mother, and I remained behind in the hotel room, while Ben was flown to Nassau with a couple of fellows from there.

It was a small, twin-engine plane. Conversation flowed as they traveled over the gorgeous blue Caribbean waters to the capital city. Just as the island came into view, one of the propeller engines began to sputter and went out. As it quit, the plane started to list, with the nose up and the tail down. The pilot began grappling with various controls and finally admitted, "We're in trouble." But Ben had already deduced that and had gone into deep prayer. As they neared the runway, they could see the fire trucks standing by for the inevitable. The pilot then shared his plan. He said, "When we get close to the runway, here's what I'm going to do. Since the plane tends to list upward, I'm going to shut off the power. The plane will then go into a dive. When the plane is close to the ground, I will power up again, and the plane's tendency to list upward will reorient the aircraft to a manageable landing posture, and we should be able to land smoothly." Ben, not quite questioning the guy's sanity, asked in a querulous voice, "Have you ever done anything like this before?" The pilot honestly replied, "No, but it's the best strategy I can come up with." Ben had his doubts, but continued in prayer. The emergency maneuver worked, and about fifty feet onto the runway the other engine sputtered to a stop. (God answers prayer!)

Several years later when Ben was visiting Alaska for a speaking engagement, he got in a little early. He was offered the opportunity to view some of the local sights by air to pass the time, and how could he resist? Alaska is known for its unparalleled, breathtaking beauty, and this was his first time visiting there.

He strapped himself into the seat of the single-engine prop plane and they were off: soaring between mountains, swooping down between them to take a closer look at the local animals and unique rock formations, banking left or right to take in another spectacular view.

But the enjoyment was short-lived. The calm tranquillity suddenly and abruptly turned ominous as the clouds swiftly darkened and closed in on the small plane. Without special instruments to navigate in cloud cover, the trip seemed doomed to disaster. Neither the pilot nor Ben could see anything but clouds. Ben could only hold on as the pilot put his plan into action. He made the plane climb at as steep an angle as it could without stalling. He figured they needed to get out of the valley they had been exploring as soon as possible before they hit something. Upward they climbed, gaining height, but not knowing if they might graze or take a full hit from the side of the mountain unexpectedly, because they had no visuals. After several anxious moments of climbing, they could finally see a small break in the clouds . . . with blue sky in it! When they reached that sky, they saw that they had missed the mountain— by about three feet! Air they didn't even realize they had been hold- ing whooshed out of their lungs. From that point on they made sure they stayed in a part of the sky where they could see clearly for a distance, and they carefully found their way back to base without further incident.

The final close call in flight was on a commercial plane on the way to New York. Ben and I were traveling together this time. The plane was an average-size jet and everything was going well. We even caught a little nap.

All of a sudden, without warning the plane began a precipitous fall. Nose down, full speed ahead . . . there was definitely some screaming. (But it wasn't coming from Ben or me!) Ben's first hope- ful thought was, "Since it's winter and there's snow on the ground, maybe it will cushion the crash." I wasn't awake enough to realize the danger—I hadn't had much sleep that week, and this was my first opportunity. A jerk of the plane woke me out of my stupor and the nightmare was alive. The screaming of my dreams was echoing about the cabin. Shouts of "We're going to die!" were repeated by several passengers at extremely high decibel levels.

Almost as suddenly, about two thousand feet from the ground, the plane leveled out and began a slow climb back to the assigned flight altitude. For several minutes there was silence. Other pas- sengers on the plane began to relate similar experiences and men- tioned that usually the pilot will attempt to calm the passengers with the reason for unexpected "detours" or changes in flight pat- terns. But nothing was coming from the cockpit. A pilot who was sitting behind us said he'd never been in that kind of a rapid descent before, that this was truly out of the ordinary. Five minutes . . . ten minutes went by, and still no word from the cockpit. After about fifteen minutes the loudspeaker crackled, followed by a shaky female voice, breathlessly exclaiming, "I . . . don't know . . . what that . . . was . . . but . . . I'm . . . sure . . . glad . . . we got out of it!"

Ben simply concluded that it wasn't time for us to go yet. But why were we being spared? We knew Ben had already done important work as a surgeon, but we began to wonder if something else was lined up for us. What it was, we didn't know.

Waking America

Then in 2011, Ben felt the urge to write a book about how special our country is. So many people had become preoccupied with the lifestyles of the rich and famous and all the reality TV shows, and had forgotten how wonderful and unique America is. Our founders had a unique vision for this country, and Abraham Lincoln encapsulated it in his Gettysburg Address, that it would be "of the people, by the people, for the people." Our predecessors were willing to do whatever it took to maintain that vision. Ben felt called to wake up our country to the beauty of the vision. The book was *America the Beautiful*. And instead of using professional cowriters as he had done previously, he asked me to help. It was so inspiring for me to rediscover the founders and their ideas for this country in my research. And we know God had a hand in this, because a book that could conceivably take a year or two to write was complete in six months!

In the meantime, although Ben was still on staff at Hopkins, operating, lecturing, et cetera, he felt called to speak more and more about the unique experiment that is America. And he followed that call. Now when he would address the audiences at his speaking engagements, he would include in his talk certain specifics of American history and the opportunities this experiment provided for all.

Ben had been cancer free for ten years when we collaborated on our first book, covering this topic. He had written four books by that time: *Gifted Hands, Think Big, The Big Picture,* and *Take the Risk.* My writing background had been reporting stories for our scholarship Web site, commenting on awards banquets and reading room openings, and I had written several articles for our church periodicals. I wasn't an expert, but Ben figured that working with someone in-house might be easier than hiring a writer. With the easy and quick access for sharing ideas, I believe he might have been right.

Things were going well with our arrangement. He liked using the dictating machine, and I would do research and editing. We were within three or four chapters of completing the manuscript when things just became ridiculously busy at the hospital, and writing came to a halt. He couldn't find time to get to his part, and if he couldn't do his part, I couldn't follow up with mine.

Well, he had agreed about a year before this to go on a cruise as a "celebrity" to help raise funds for prostate cancer research. We couldn't get any writing done for several weeks before the cruise with the heavy workload at the hospital, and our deadline was the last day of the cruise. So I schlepped books and my computer, and he had his computer with its dictation app, and off we went.

We always travel with carry-ons only, because at too many critical times in our travel life, our checked bags didn't make it to our destination in time for us to use the clothes. For a six-day cruise, can you believe we each had only the two carry-ons? He packed several shirts, shorts, and slacks in his roll-around, and his computer and papers went into his briefcase. On the other hand I, being female, needed twelve outfits. You know how it is on a vacation, casual during the day while you perspire all you want, and then dressy at night, no sweat allowed. Somehow, with the method of rolling clothes as tight as possible and securing the rolls with scarves or rubber bands, I got twelve outfits, several books, and my computer in my roll-around and tote bag.

Here is how our schedule worked: during the day, Ben was on the balcony of our stateroom doing his dictating, while I was editing and following up on research items in the cabin at my computer. Unfortunately, despite all that attention to what went in our suitcases I had forgotten my computer cord. (Actually I think it fell out at home when I pushed the clothes down hard so I could close the suitcase.) I really needed that cord! To my relief, one of the travelers in our group had the same computer and was willing to let me use the cord during the day, while he used it each night. We'd make the exchange at breakfast in the morning and at dinner in the evening. God is good again!

This particular cruise was in the Caribbean, and we had visited most of the islands before (including during that working trip where Ben spoke and the kids and I played), so it wasn't as sacrificial a trip as one might think. During the day, we worked. In the evenings we socialized with the group for dinner. And then it was back to the grind for a couple of hours before turning in. As the week unfolded and it was looking like we were going to make it, we actually did have a chance to go on a couple of land excursions.

As beautiful as the islands are, and as lovely as the cruise was, there was absolutely nothing more satisfying and pleasurable than hitting the "send" button when we finished that manuscript. We were working our tails off to get it done in time, and man, what a feeling of satisfaction it was to have it complete and off to the publisher. We finished shortly before the cruise was over. God is great! He got us through.

Pool Shark

All of this book writing was serious business, but don't think we didn't find ways to have fun at the same time. While taking a break from writing on the cruise, I discovered the ship had pool tables. Then I saw a notice about a pool tournament, and I was psyched. I knew Ben would be excited about the tables, too, and I figured that he might not mind competing in the tournament. I wasn't sure he had ever participated in one before. When I found one of the crew who was involved with activities, she responded to my questions with answers that fit our schedule, so we went back at the appropriate time to "let the games begin."

You might wonder how a pool table would work aboard ship when it's constantly moving. The plaque on the wall described the mechanics in detail, how the tabletop was balanced on a ball bearing the size of a grape and signals were sent from each corner of the table to the Earth's center to keep it parallel and level with it. But looks can be deceiving. When the ship would pitch this way and that, the table would stay still, parallel to the Earth's center. But because the players were moving with the ship, our point of reference made us feel like the table was moving!

There were several guys playing, a professor from the British Isles, a businessman (who happened to have grandchildren) from Puerto Rico, and another businessman from South America. You bet I was excited when I saw that there were five trophies and only five players. I figured even if I came in last, it wouldn't matter, I'd still get to take one of those neat little trophies home. And when I thought about the other contestants, I felt I shouldn't play as hard as I might. Guys have egos, each one would love to have a story about playing pool on the ship, and most guys really don't like to be beaten by a girl, so I didn't concentrate like I might have. It didn't matter so much if I didn't win, but I figured the guys would appreciate it more than I would.

Things went reasonably well. They were all good players, but Ben was in excellent form. Some games were close, but in the end the champion of the one and only shipboard tournament was none other than Dr. Ben! He graciously shook hands with everyone, and the ship's representative handed out trophies to everyone—but me! After all that sacrifice, I didn't get my trophy. And I worked hard for it by letting everyone else win! (That wasn't too hard, because they really were better than I was. But still!) I felt like I was cheated. "Not fair," I fumed to myself. I guess the moral of this story is: All is fair in love, war . . . and pool on board ship!

Determination—and a Sign

We managed to get through the book writing process and found that the book was well received and increased Ben's opportunities to speak about America. Life at the hospital was no less tense, though, and Ben was still keeping a grueling schedule when we were home. Then his life was spared one more time, and it seemed like the Lord wanted to rouse our attention once again.

On a typical morning in March 2012, Ben was driving to work in his favorite car, a royal blue BMW, listening to the morning news, alert and planning the day in his mind. Exiting the expressway, turning onto the familiar eastbound Monument Street, he motored past the park and Dunbar High School. The light at Caroline Street had just turned green, and as he entered the intersection, without any warning, *BAM!* The car jerked wildly with the impact and went sideways as the airbag deployed, knocking Ben's glasses off.

Several moments later, as the shock wore off, his first thought was that he was grateful to be alive, and his second was that he needed to get to work. He started checking himself to see if everything still worked, and he was pretty sure he was fine, but he couldn't get out of the car. When the police came, they pried open the car door and found his glasses relatively quickly so he could finally see.

Ben was shaken, but he knew he had a responsibility to his patients and felt that he was stable enough to carry out his work. And he didn't want to disappoint the patients who had already had to wait a long time to get on the schedule. One of the officers offered to drive Ben the couple of blocks to work, and one of the others offered to loan Ben his phone for the day because Ben's phone had been thrown to a distant recess of the car in the accident. The woman who ran the red light was taken to the hospital.

Within moments of reaching his office, Ben received calls from the president of the hospital, the president of the university, and people from all over Hopkins Institutions. Bad news travels fast, and everyone was relieved that he was fine.

Ben had been working for more than thirty years at this point and had been considering retirement off and on for the last few. When he read an article stating the average age of death for a neurosurgeon was sixty-one, he thought that was ludicrous. So he decided to test the theory. After writing down the names of the last ten neurosurgeons he knew who were no longer around, he did the mathematical calculations and discovered that the article was right. At that point he determined that if he was still alive at that age he would retire. He felt that he didn't want to be one of those guys who stay a bit past their prime, and also, he wanted to be young enough to actually enjoy his retirement, not so old and feeble that he couldn't participate in a lot of the things he had missed over the years. He had served enough years at the hospital and felt it was a good idea for him to retire before becoming one of those statistics of doctors who die young. Besides, his burden for America was only getting stronger. We figured retirement would provide much-needed rest and give him a chance to spend more time speaking about the beauty of the American dream to its citizens.

Chapter 12

Retirement?

Ben and I had traveled to more than fifty-seven countries and all over the United States, so when he retired, we wanted to relax at home and enjoy being in one place. And he had plans! One was proving that "old people" can learn. His method of proving this was teaching himself to play the organ. All the movies he never saw that everyone always raved about, all the bestselling books people had described that he wanted to try, and visiting local amusements— he was ready to do them all! And I was looking forward to playing with an orchestra and singing in a choir again. Oh, the exciting anticipation of sleeping past five a.m., not working ten- to sixteen-hour days, and doing all the things you never had a chance to do during a demanding career. Ben was thinking he would no longer have to answer in the negative questions like "Have you seen this film?" and "Have you been to *X*?" We could hardly contain our joy as we anticipated retirement. Little did we know that we'd end up spending only about four days a month enjoying it.

A New Home

Because we would not be bound by geographical constraints, discussion arose about where we would move to enjoy retirement. Ben jokingly called our state "The People's Republic of Maryland" because the taxes had become quite burdensome, and he was ready to go someplace where the taxes were lower. We *knew* we wanted to move from Maryland. The state is beautiful, with lovely parks and reservoirs, and Ben had enjoyed working with the many intellectually gifted and dedicated people at Hopkins. We also had belonged to great church families, our charity was based in the state, and we had developed great relationships with the board of education and other charities. But it was still a high tax state. When the last governor while we were residents came into office, the state was ranked number twenty-five among business-friendly states. In a few years, it was down to number forty-nine due to the governor's ever-increasing taxation system. The latest tax he introduced while we were there was a "rain tax." Anyone who had a roof or a paved surface (driveway, parking pad, or lot) had to pay extra for the water runoff. That was the proverbial straw that broke the camel's back. (A new administration repealed it about a year after we moved, however.)

The search for a friendlier tax state ended when we looked into Florida's system. And in December 2012, I was elected to go to Florida to find our new domicile, because we were in between books and Ben was still working full time at Hopkins. So for a few weekends in that busiest of months, online searches and trips to Florida were my focus, in between performances and scheduling special music for church.

Florida homes have their own special beauty. We loved our home in Maryland, a brick colonial with tall white pillars and a drive-through portico, but Florida homes have an airiness about them. Many have lots of glass to take advantage of the gorgeous vistas found in warmer states, including waving palm trees and perfectly blue skies with puffy clouds close enough to almost touch.

Working with a Realtor friend of a friend, on a typical day I would get to between three and five houses. When Ben and I spoke on the phone at night to compare our days, he'd get the full report. After the third trip down, he traveled with me over the Christmas holiday to check things out for himself. Staying with a friend, we went house hunting every day to narrow down the choices.

We wanted five bedrooms so that we could have family reunions with enough space for each of our sons' families and a room for grandkids; I was hoping to have a circular drive so no one would have to back out and so we could see cars coming; Ben needed a study, something we didn't have in Maryland, so he could continue to write; and of course we needed room for a pool table.

In addition, as was mentioned before, one of Ben's dreams for a retirement activity was to teach himself to play the organ. So we needed to allow room for this instrument as well as a piano. (Our Friday night tradition for decades has had me on the piano playing praise music while he studies to prepare the lesson he would teach the following morning. It's a great way to relax.)

With the Realtor's help, we had narrowed the possible homes down to three and were feeling fairly well settled in our choices as we awaited our flight in the Palm Beach Airport. When Ben heard someone call his name, turning around he met the accountant from Maryland who audits our charity. After catching up a little, the auditor asked what brought us to Florida, and we shared that information, including the places where we thought we might buy.

He then mentioned the development where he lives and said how happy he was with that neighborhood.

So when we got home and I had access to a computer, my curiosity got the best of me and I Googled his housing development. It appeared to be as nice as any we had seen, and the Web site had a real estate section. One home in particular really caught my eye. I couldn't believe how fabulous this place was. It contained all the elements we were searching for in a home, but had so many extras that were details we had only dared to dream of having. Think of it: a home theater room with a big screen and three smaller screens above it! While you watch your favorite game, you can also keep an eye on the competition! Faux painted marble walls and columns, two-story-high ceilings with glass on three sides for breathtaking views of the golf course, backyard and fountain-accessorized pool and Jacuzzi! And tray ceilings! In the photos the home appeared to be in excellent shape as well.

When I called Ben in to look, he was possibly even more impressed than I was. He called a friend in Florida and asked him to go see if it was as nice as it looked. Ben knew that this friend, who lives in Wellington, would be predisposed not to like the property because he would prefer that we live closer to his family. But our search committee of one came back with excitement in his voice: "Ben, this is the one!"

Before we even began the search, Ben and I had prayed about it. We figured God knew where He wanted us and would direct us to the best place. Well, He certainly did. Not only was the place itself special and gorgeous, but the previous owners had left most of their furniture. Each bedroom had at least one bed and linens. Each bathroom had towels. The dining room set was carved hardwood, possibly mahogany. And the chairs were covered in expensive embroidered silk fabric. The windows all had blinds or drapes. The theater room had very cushiony soft, comfortable seats and the sound system was like the one we had installed in our home in Maryland, with speakers throughout the house. And the price was amazingly low for all the value we were getting. The owners were motivated sellers.

We didn't get a chance to go back and actually see the house in person before we bought it. When a gift like that drops in your lap, you just say, "Thank you, Jesus!" and keep going. So our friend thoroughly checked out the house, negotiated for us, and when we returned to Florida at the end of January 2013, our first stop was at the title company, where we signed the deal. We were so excited to be able to spend our first night in our brand-new home, in what was for us a brand-new state.

Although Florida is known for its hot climate, that night we got a big surprise when the outside temperature dropped to 50. Not a bad temperature during the day if you have a jacket and the sun is shining, but inside the house at night the chill was definitely shiver producing. Waking up to cold in the middle of the night is not fun, but I recalled seeing extra blankets in one of the guest rooms and fortified our heat preservation tactics with those until morning. In the light of day when the drowsiness of sleep had left us and we could think more clearly, we remembered there was indeed a thermostat. And we could actually turn the heat on. Duh! So at nine a.m., we enthusiastically switched the thermostat mode to heat instead of cool, and what a joy to hear the heat coming on to rescue us.

That lasted for about three minutes.

Suddenly, an alarm went off. It was quite an impressive loud. Fortunately for us, we didn't feel as guilty as we might for setting it off, because it was nine instead of three a.m. when we first felt the chill, but in a quiet neighborhood like this, we knew we needed to get that thing turned off. It only took a few minutes for one of the security people to arrive to help. Ben and I had already been searching high and low for the turnoff, but hadn't located the unit yet. So Officer Sandy was running all over the house with us, and we finally discovered the necessary nuisance in a utility room in the garage, almost out of sight, high up in a corner. Surprisingly, we never heard complaints from any of our neighbors—nice people. Whether they were out of town or not isn't important . . . they didn't complain. The reason for the noise? The dust that had collected in the air ducts over the past year was reacting to the increase in temperature and the resulting hyperactivity of the dust motes was setting the silly alarm off.

Fortunately, that was one of the few glitches we had with our dream home, which was an answer to prayer, suited our needs perfectly, and had a tremendous backyard view with palm trees and hibiscus plants. It was a great new place to call home. All that remained was for Ben to actually retire and for us to settle in, but we barely had time to with all the speaking engagements.

Prayer Breakfast in 2013

Shortly after we bought our home but before he retired, Ben was asked to speak at the National Prayer Breakfast for 2013. Ben knew something was up. He had spoken about fifteen years ago when Bill Clinton was president, and he hadn't heard of anyone who had been the speaker for it more than once. When he asked the organizers if anyone else had spoken twice, they informed him the only one who had was Billy Graham. And Ben thought, "Well, those are very good footsteps to follow in. God, what are you up to? What do you want me to do?"

He figured God must have a special message for him to present to the American people, or he wouldn't have been put in that position, so he prayed about it. He wrote down the outline of what he thought God would want him to say. Then he prayed more and rewrote the framework. He kept rewriting it for days. It seemed one day the talk should go one way, then on another day it would turn in a completely different direction.

The night before he was to give the speech, at ten p.m. he still had the light on, reworking the speech . . . until he finally gave up and went to sleep. As the next day dawned bright and clear, so did his thoughts. He knew exactly what he should say.

The rest is history. The outpouring of support from all over the country for the content of Ben's speech was incredible. So many resonated with his unifying comments and commonsense approaches. We discovered this from e-mails, letters, and in person as Ben continued to speak all over the country to help everyone understand the serious situation our country is in. And people are still responding.

An Issue of Vision

Speaking engagement requests continued to increase, and Ben accepted every one that fit on the schedule, because our country's economic crisis was continuing to escalate. (At the penning of this book the national debt sits at more than $18.5 trillion. Easy to say, but hard to wrap your mind around this astronomical amount. To pay this off at a rate of $10 million per day, every day, 365 days per year would take more than five thousand years!) He traveled to between four and six states each week. When he officially announced his retirement, he was free to speak even more.

It was a tough schedule, but as he responds to any such concerns, "It's not brain surgery!" So he kept going and going. Then he began to notice how sometimes he had trouble reading signs; more often than not, things would be blurry. An appointment at Johns Hopkins Wilmer Eye Institute revealed cataracts in both eyes. Surgery was needed, and I tried to travel more with him then to help, at least until he could get on the surgical schedule to take care of these latest health issues.

Trying to schedule surgery with such a demanding travel itinerary was truly a challenge. But finally a date was set for December. The proverbial light at the end of the tunnel was on its way. But as fate would have it, in late November his own surgeon got sick. Several more weeks went by before he could even think about trying to do something about his eyes. Then finally he found out from a friend about the Bascom Palmer Eye Institute in Miami. Everyone he spoke to about it gave rave reviews, praising the doctors, the service, and the results. And we also discovered that Bascom Palmer is ranked the number one ophthalmology department in the entire country. We were way beyond relieved to find they could get him on the schedule.

Ben went through all the preliminaries and the day of surgery came quickly (in between speaking engagements again). The concierge service was more than helpful and things went very smoothly. In less than an hour, the surgery was complete and Ben was rolled back into the temporary room that had been reserved for him, where I had been waiting. They had only used local anesthetic, so he was awake. Because he had tuned the television to his favorite news source when we arrived, I had left it on that station, figuring he'd appreciate seeing some of his favorite people once he returned. Right after the nurses transferred him from the gurney to the hospital bed, he asked me, "Are my glasses on my face? I can see the TV!" The sensation around his eyes had not returned yet, so he was absolutely certain his glasses were on because he could see so clearly. Just think about it . . . he had been bound to wearing glasses since it was discovered in grade school that he couldn't see the chalkboard. And now, no more glasses! Gaining complete vision in retirement doesn't happen for everyone. I don't think there has ever been a happier camper. Our prayer was that Americans would regain their moral vision, too.

Come Again

After his speech, Ben began thinking of writing a book to amplify the themes he had shared at the prayer breakfast. He felt more and more inspired to try to help our citizenry gain a better understanding of the metamorphosis occurring in our nation. Not only was the vision of our founding fathers slipping, but radical changes were happening right before our eyes in every state and most if not all departments of the federal government, without appearing to attract the attention of the public. People needed to wake up and remember that the government that was supposed to be of, by, and for the people was rapidly becoming of, by, and for the government. Ben felt the call again and followed the urge to compose another book.

This one would be about the state of the Union. After checking with several publishers, we signed with Penguin to write *One Nation*. Due to the urgency of getting the word out, the time line for writing it was even shorter. This book was due to be released shortly after the next National Prayer Breakfast, and Penguin scheduled a book tour to maximize the book's effect: twenty-eight cities in nine days! The schedule was grueling for Ben and the logistics team, but it was effective.

The bookstores had really done their advertising well. The tour bus with Ben and me on it would pull up to a bookstore, a couple of the guys would get out and set up for the book signing, and Ben would be ushered in among a cheering throng. No event had fewer than five hundred people standing in line. Ben's exposure to each person or group was limited to five to ten seconds, because the allotted time for the signing was only an hour, so he didn't have much time to talk. One of the tour people would help with getting the books to the correct page for a signature, another would be ready with a camera to snap a photo, and another would position bookstore guests for photos with Ben and keep the line moving. Ben was his gracious self throughout the process. He always tries to think of others and didn't want anyone to be left out, so he would sign as quickly as possible in order to accommodate everyone who had shown up, always maintaining a smile on his face and sharing courteous words when time would allow.

Because I wasn't required to sit and sign, I could do one of my favorite things: browse the books in the store. Normally, I wouldn't have time to visit bookstores and browse, so this was a special treat. But I also kept myself available to chat about the book. Because the time each autograph seeker had with Ben was so limited, I felt perhaps I could take some of the sting out of the limitation and answer any questions they might have. Sharing about the book was fun. I loved talking about the "friends" we had made during our research; the more I had learned about the founding fathers, the more I admired their determination and tenacity in developing and maintaining a country of, by, and for the people.

The Message Versus the Messenger

Some people would get puffed up with the amount of attention Ben was receiving. It would be easy to become self-centered and overly concerned with image. But Ben seemed to stay pretty grounded, even when he had to repeatedly face a somewhat embarrassing situation.

Ben was on the speakers' circuit almost daily, so there wasn't much time for anything else. Although he was up to date with his dental work, at one appointment his dentist had put in the temporaries that were to be replaced with permanents in three weeks. But his speaking commitments to a rather large number of organizations for the weeks following that dental visit filled his calendar, and he couldn't bring himself to disappoint the people by canceling or rescheduling. So he kept going. Three months later, while he was at such an event eating pizza, one of his favorite foods, one of his front temporary teeth came out. It was only moments before he was scheduled to speak, so nothing could be done about this situation until after his speech. With his usual aplomb, he took to the stage, made a joke about it, and continued with his address. Fortunately, there were dentists present who were willing to work on his teeth afterward, even though it was in the evening.

The next morning, during breakfast before he got up to speak, he was thoroughly enjoying his grits. (Our Sunday morning tradition was always grits, eggs, and veggie sausage patties.) As he was eating, his other front tooth decided to join the spoon and poor Ben was missing a front tooth just prior to speaking again. He joked about it and carried right on with his speech, figuring that the message was more important than the appearance of the messenger. In his typical manner Ben wasn't thinking about himself, but about the fact that many people had come to the event to hear the message and it needed to be delivered. Again, the good fortune of another dentist's willingness to repair the damage benefited Ben (he even came in on his day off), and he proceeded to the next event after the requisite repairs were swiftly completed.

A Namesake

June 9, 2015, was an enormously special day for Ben and me. It was the culmination of hopes, dreams, dedication, hard work, determination, sweat equity, and sacrifice. That date was the inaugural graduation of the model experimental high school in Detroit that had been named after Ben, the Ben Carson High School of Science and Medicine. It was just four years ago that the special honor had been bestowed on him. The opening of the new high school, which would focus on developing health care professionals and those interested in pursuing careers in science, seemed like only yesterday. Naming the school after one of Detroit's own successful native sons was done to inspire the next generation to achieve in similar ways.

This self-governing school of the Detroit public school system has a special vision to prepare all students to be leaders and agents of change who positively impact their world. Its location, across the street from Harper-Hutzel and Detroit Receiving hospitals, means that BCHS students interested in careers in science and/or medicine can intern there as well as shadow physicians in the clinical and research areas. They even have opportunities at several other partnering medical facilities, including Wayne State University, Michigan State University College of Osteopathic Medicine, the Detroit Medical Center, and the Henry Ford Health System.

After four years of industrious study, these young people had completed the requirements for their diplomas and would have the distinction of being the Ben Carson High School of Science and Medicine's inaugural graduating class. The ceremony was held in the historic Detroit Opera House.

Students and educators alike were excited that Ben was the commencement speaker. How often do graduates have the opportunity to hear their school's namesake speak at their graduation? The event was truly significant to Ben as well. He was back in his hometown, which had suffered almost complete bankruptcy but was now on the rebound. Detroit was like a microcosm of the nation. This was what he had been speaking about for the last few years. And he had declared his run for the office of president of the United States just one month earlier only a few blocks away. He felt the weight of that responsibility, as well as the weight of concern for the future of these young people, as he stood onstage. But most of all he took pride in their accomplishments and, along with his nostalgia for his own teen years in Detroit, was full of hope that they would help our country move forward. As the Navy Junior ROTC marched in with the flags and posted the colors, Ben couldn't help but recall his involvement with the ROTC when he was a high school student in the same city more than forty years ago. This ROTC team brought back memorable images of the challenges and the triumphs that helped to make him who he is today.

The school had four valedictorians, to our amazement. Four students had achieved at the highest academic level possible in order to hold that title. Four valedictorians! The emcee of the ceremony commented that he had been to all of the schools in Detroit in his career, and not one of them, even those with large classes, had more than two. And this class was one of the smaller ones, with ninety-eight graduates.

In addition, there were two salutatorians who were responsible for introducing Ben, India Amos and Kiara Marshall. In their presentation they included his rise from humble beginnings to his stature as a world-class neurosurgeon and a candidate for president of the United States.

When it was time for the four valedictorians to deliver their addresses, they drew close to the lectern and spoke in turn. The first, Camera Edgar, spoke on Ben's philosophy that "the person who has the most to do with what happens to you is you." The second, Shaila Moore, talked about how "the sky doesn't have to be the limit," concluding with "You can soar past the sky!" The third, Nayeem Latif, spoke appreciatively of the relationships she was able to develop with classmates and mentors who each had a part in spurring her on to excellence. And finally, Vicenta Vargas charged his classmates to "seize the day" and make the most of each and every moment. Each one of them inspired hope, confidence, and determination among their class members to become "the best you can be."

When counselor Millicynt Horton announced that the class of 2015 had earned more than $3.6 million in scholarships, with many of the recipients having been awarded a full ride, the cheers rose. An impressive six patriotic students were becoming active duty military, and more than 50 percent of the graduates would be entering the field of medicine.

As Ben approached the lectern, the enthusiastic cheers echoed to the rafters. Recalling that forty-six years ago he was in the same place they were, wondering what the future would hold, he reassured them that the foundation of a good Detroit high school education was everything he had needed to succeed, taking him all kinds of places, even to fifty-seven different countries. He called Detroit a "great city that is in the process of becoming great again." Taking us back to his formative years, he expressed his gratitude for a mother who never accepted excuses. Because of that attitude, although he joined the ROTC a semester late, he never allowed any excuse to get in the way, and he achieved his goal of becoming city executive officer for the city of Detroit, the highest rank in the city a student can achieve, placing him over all the other schools in the entire metropolis.

He cautioned the students to beware of naysayers, using the example of his medical school adviser who told him that he wasn't cut out to be a doctor. When someone tells you something like that, he said, remember that they are speaking from their own experience, about what they can't do. They really can't speak for what you can do. Only you have control over what you can do. That adviser caused him to rethink his learning strategies, discover the best way he learned, and apply those principles to his studies. Once he did that, the rest of medical school was a snap.

Finally, Ben told the students:

> Do what you need to succeed and do it in conjunction with God's will. We have a proud tradition of being people of faith. . . . Think about the flag and the Pledge of Allegiance, how "In God We Trust" is in all our courtrooms, on our founding documents, and on our money.

Don't allow people to tell you you can't talk about this or that. And it's okay to live by godly principles . . . caring for your fellow man . . . and having values and principles to live by. And if you do these things, not only will you be successful, but we as a people will truly have one nation under God with liberty and justice for all.

Principal Brenda Belcher's remarks followed in appreciation for all the efforts that went into the success of the students and the program, and expressed her hope that they would all have a lifelong connection with BCHS. Her last charge was for them not to quit just because something becomes difficult: "You only have this life to live . . . challenge yourself!"

As the students came forward and proudly crossed the stage when their names were called, those of us on the dais were honored to shake their hands and congratulate them.

A restful retirement? We've heard of that concept. Since Ben's announcement in May 2015, the schedule has become even more hectic. We travel constantly, usually together, which makes the busy schedule a bit more tolerable. Ben has shared the fact that running for public office was not on his bucket list, and it certainly wasn't on mine. I was so happy to actually have a husband whom I saw for more than a few minutes per day. But the people spoke up, asking him to run and backing that request with a lot of support. Ben said, "Lord, you know I don't want to do this, but as long as You open the doors, I will walk through them. If you close the doors, I'll gladly sit down." God has been opening doors like crazy. In the first three weeks, the team raised more than $2 million. In the first month, more than forty thousand donations came in, most of which were around $50. About one million Facebook fans signed up in the first month as well. By the end of the summer he had 3.5 million Facebook fans, over half a million donors, and several huge donors were seeking him out, even though he has broadcast that he will not sell favors. And the polls show that he is in the top tier. I can't argue with this.

For me the decision came down to my grandchildren. How could you not do all you can to ensure these innocent ones have at least the same opportunities and freedoms that we have enjoyed? I feel so privileged to have remained married to my college sweetheart for over forty years. Ben and I have been through a lot together. We've gone through deep waters of tragedy and have rejoiced in God's special blessings. We've sometimes hurt each other and journeyed through forgiveness. And we have laughed a lot.

When BJ was born fast and furiously, after pretty much delivering the baby myself, I had to run around to find a clip for the placenta, something you wouldn't normally ask a new mom to do. We are used to dealing with the crazy and the unexpected and have found that difficulty has always brought us closer to each other.

I liked Ben Carson the day that I met him and have loved him for more than forty years. As we head forward into the unknown once more, I thank God for putting us together. We look forward to the next adventure as we follow God's lead.

Acknowledgments

Thank you to my dear family, who put up with the insane writing schedule and shared their stories quickly, and Ben's brother, Curtis Carson, for delightful and insightful childhood memories. For those of you who prayed for me as well, thank you! Those prayers were certainly answered! Ben, of course this couldn't have happened at all without you. And your patient, caring, thoughtful, and loving ways still astound me! Thanks also to the folks at Sentinel, especially Bria Sandford for all her hard work, and Kaushik Viswanath for doing such a great job with the photos. I am grateful also to Sealy Yates for his help and encouragement and to Marty Weber for his valuable insights.

My heartfelt appreciation also goes to representatives of Ben's medical family at Johns Hopkins Hospital (JHH) and elsewhere whose input provided profound enlightenment on that huge facet of Ben's life:

Carol James, Ben's Senior Physician Assistant (JHH)

Mary K. Conover-Walker, Neurosurgery Nurse Practitioner (JHH)

Audrey Jones, Ben's Office Manager (JHH)

Dr. Henry Brem, current Chief of Neurosurgery (JHH)

Dr. Pablo Recinos, current Section Head of Skull Base Surgery at Cleveland Clinic

Dr. Violette Renard Recinos, current Section Head of Pediatric Neurosurgery at Cleveland Clinic

Dr. Patti Vining, recently retired Director of Pediatric Neurology (JHH)

and last but certainly not least, I must heartily thank Dr. Donlin Long, who served as the Chief of Neurosurgery at Johns Hopkins for twenty-seven years, gently but quite capably shaping the next generation of neurosurgeons and Ben's longtime mentor, for his extremely generous input.

And there's just one more "individual" whom I owe quite a lot of thanks, and that's God. To finish my first solo book in only four weeks is still amazing to me, especially when the writing schedule was three thousand words per day, and some days I could barely get past two hundred! He got me through! God is truly awesome!